FORERUNNERS COURAGEOUS
Stories of Frontier Florida

FORERUNNERS COURAGEOUS
Stories of Frontier Florida

LeRoy Collins

Drawings By Wallace Hughes

Colcade Publishers, Inc., 1971

Printed in the United States of America

Library of Congress Catalog Card Number: 76–185182

Colcade Publishers, Inc.
Tallahassee, Florida

DEDICATION

To those who love Florida, not just for what it is, but for what it ought to be; and who with open minds and generous hearts strive to make their dreams come true.

Contents

Foreword

By Ed H. Price, Jr.*

As I VIEW it this book has a strong significance beyond the history-telling that the author claims as his prime objective.

It is important also to Floridians for what it tells them about LeRoy Collins and to Americans for its insights into his kind of political leadership.

The history books dryly list Collins as the thirty-third governor of Florida, having previously held this and that office, who later did thus and so. His portrait in the Capitol at Tallahassee is much like those of the men who served as governor before and after.

But histories and official portraits have a way of omitting the essence of men, and the essence of LeRoy Collins is that he practiced the politics of unity. He brought people together in Florida and America in a time when mutual respect and understanding were as difficult to achieve as today.

Florida was in turmoil when Collins became governor in 1955. The year before, the U.S. Supreme Court had discarded the evil institution of state-enforced school segre-

---

* Ed H. Price Jr. is executive vice president of Tropicana Products Inc. of Bradenton. He is currently chairman of the Florida Citrus Commission and president of the Florida State Chamber of Commerce. He served two terms in the Florida Senate, winning numerous awards, and as a member of Florida's university Board of Control. In 1971 he received the Distinguished Citizen Award of Manatee County.

xi

gation. The difficult times of Florida's rapid population
growth were just beginning. And state government labored
under the iron hand of the most malapportioned legislature
in the whole United States.

Collins brought to the Florida of 1955 the ability to help
people understand that they had more in common than
their differences. He challenged Floridians to give their
best and to expect the best from others. He gave them an
example of courage in public office, a willingness to sacrifice momentary popularity for greater moral and ethical
principle.

This book shows one reason why Collins possessed the
ability to unify. I believe it was partially because of his
deep sense of humanity and history. LeRoy Collins knows
what he is and who he is. His past is a part of his present,
and his future. He knows where he is going because he
knows where he has been.

> "God, help me see
> Beyond the tear
> That needs drying,
> Also the cause of the crying."

Given this quality of unity, it was natural that Collins
was asked by the President in 1964 to fill the impossible
job as Director of the U.S. Community Relations Service,
a kind of national fire department against racial outbursts.
It also was natural that Collins should give up his position
as president of the National Association of Broadcasters to
accept—at great personal sacrifice.

The climate in America was one of tension and con-
fusion. Civil rights legislation was untested. A new pattern
of racial confrontation had emerged. The nation's new
fire chief was truly the man in the middle, placed between
two great historical forces, armed only with the power of
persuasion.

Collins's sense of history now served the nation. "I have
never known another man of whom it could be more truly

said that he is a man of principle," said Secretary of Commerce John T. Connor of Collins. "His ideals, his integrity, his innate ability to know instantly the right thing to do, have been a guide and inspiration to all of us who worked with him."

There are other factors in the complex explanation of Collins's impact on Florida. One was the youth he at first brought to public service. He was only 25 when elected in 1934 from Leon County to the Florida House of Representatives. After three terms there, he went to the State Senate in 1940. He was re-elected senator three times, despite an interruption when he resigned to join the Navy in World War II. As a legislator he was an effective leader winning top honors in both the Allen Morris awards and those of the *St. Petersburg Times.*

After Florida Gov. Dan McCarty died in office in 1953, his close friend LeRoy Collins ran to fill the unexpired term. Collins was a young reformer, emphasizing Florida's potential. He startled many in the state with the high moral tone of his first inaugural address:

"I want the people of Florida to understand that progress in business, industry and human welfare can only go so far with a ward-healing, back-scratching, self-promoting political system. . . Government cannot live by taxes alone or by jobs alone or even by roads alone. Governments must have qualities of the spirit. Truth and justice and unselfish service are some of these. Without these qualities there is no worthwhile leadership, and we grapple and grope in a moral wilderness."

Little did Floridians know how these courageous words would be challenged in the years ahead.

Collins carried his reform recommendations to the Legislature and it responded, writing into law three-fourths of his proposals. A merit system for state employes was started, as was a central purchasing plan. He sponsored a broad reorganization of State agencies to achieve higher efficiency,

A strong beginning was made in general constitutional revision and reapportionment. A development commission
was created, and the state's elaborate system of community
colleges was developed. The turnpike down the east coast
was built as well as expressways for major cities.

It was the race for re-election in 1956 that brought the
toughest test to Collins's unifying leadership. Under court
pressure, racial tensions in Florida were high. The state
was deciding the direction of its future. Some candidates
shouted defiance. Collins calmly counseled moderation. He
swamped five opposition candidates to become the only
Florida governor ever to win a first primary victory.

Now began the transformation of the Southerner who,
while accepting segregation, repeatedly had advised against
attacking the courts and abandoning the public schools.
In his inaugural address of 1957, Collins said he did not
know "the ultimate answer" for school desegregation. But
he did know it would do no good to defy the Supreme
Court, "an essential institution for the preservation of our
form of government." He did know that violence and dis-
order were not the answer. He knew that hate was not
the answer.

Collins said he didn't know the answer in 1957, but he
did. He ended his address with a quotation from the hymn
"Once to Every Man and Nation," by James Russell
Lowell:

> "New occasions teach new duties,
> Time makes ancient good uncouth;
> They must upward still and onward
> Who would keep abreast of truth."

When the sit-in demonstrations swept through Florida
lunch counters in 1960, Collins again urged moderation.
He said merchants legally (at that time) could serve
whomever they wished, but that he considered it "unfair
and morally wrong" to serve blacks in some departments
and to refuse them in others. No other Southern governor

would dare utter such words. Again, this was a moral stance requiring political courage. Collins had the "innate ability to know instantly the right thing to do" and the reaction was generally favorable both in Florida and the nation.

During this full term, Collins was elected chairman of the National Governors' Conference and the Southern Governors' Conference, the only governor ever to hold both jobs at once. He also was president of the National Council of State Governments, chairman of the Southern Regional Education Board and a member of the Commission on Goals and Higher Education in the South.

Collins became well known nationally for his cool evenhandedness in presiding as permanent chairman over the Democratic National Convention of 1960 which nominated John F. Kennedy for president. For a time before the convention, his name was mentioned as a potential vice presidential nominee. That bid, of course, went to another Southerner, Lyndon B. Johnson.

I hope young people will read this book. I hope they will be inspired by it to cultivate their own sense of history. I hope the leaders among the young will find an example in the career of LeRoy Collins. As governor, he encouraged many young people to join actively in the challenging work of building a better state and nation. His inspiration and encouragement led me into public life.

The national agenda that Collins listed in 1966, his last year as under secretary of Commerce, remains unmet:

1. Making equal opportunity a reality in America.
2. The elimination of the scourge of poverty.
3. The elimination of pollution in our natural environment.
4. The achievement of sustained national economic growth, avoiding cycles of boom and depression.
5. Development of a firm basis for world peace.

Yet the tool Collins used in Florida and Washington is too often neglected:

"Nothing is beyond our capabilities. If America will face its needs with knowledge of their meaning and dimensions, with a UNITY of purpose for meeting them, with a will to work and sacrifice in such efforts, then we cannot fail."

"God, help me see
Beyond the tear
That needs drying,
Also the cause of the crying."

Preface

THE STORIES I tell here excite me and I hope they will excite the reader. I am deeply proud of our State's history and I so want this book to make a contribution, even if only a slight one, to its telling. In every story with a historic base, I have sought to keep within provable facts. Where it may seem that I have strayed, it has been likely because: (1) In some instances, history does not supply detail and I have substituted what I sincerely feel would be logical, taking into account all known facts; and (2) Where historians have left a range of choices of inconsistencies, I have taken the one I like best.

The U. S. Weather Bureau a few years back, in predicting the weather, used such terms as "probability," "likely," etc. Whatever the weather predicted, so often it turned out wrong in the public mind because a "probability" was accepted as a prediction of what would happen. Some genius then devised the plan now used of rating what is to happen in percentages, such as a "20% chance of rain." This way, the weatherman can't be wrong because if it rains, the occurrence falls in the predicted 20% range; if it does not, the clear weather falls in the predicted 80% range. Either way, it turns out just like he said.

So I say this: my book is 90% authentic history. If a reader finds something that isn't, don't worry, it will just be a part of the other 10%.

There are four logical divisions of the book. Chapters I though VI are stories from early territorial times through the Civil War period.

Then, there is an "Interlude" which embraces a few things I have written at one time or another. They are grouped under the subtitle of "Reflections of a Part-time Beachcomber." The first, (a), and last, (e), are autobiographical; those in between are largely philosophical and, hopefully, inspirational. Chapters VII through X relate to the Spanish-American War times and turn of the century.

Chapter XI, "The House of Call," has a scope which spans the whole time, from territorial days to the present. I want here to give the reader an interpretation of Richard Keith Call, the man and his works, which I feel were truly monumental.

If there was any single individual who contributed most in the development of Florida, both as a United States territory and as a state in the early formative years, I think Call deserves the distinction.

As a military leader, he led those who first made the territory safe for settlement. As a member of the Territorial Council, he was in the forefront of those establishing a rule of law to govern the new frontier. As Delegate of the Territory to the United States Congress, he fostered congressional authorization for the establishment of the territorial capital at Tallahassee and vast internal improvements. Also in this role, he led the early entrepreneurs in encouraging high-level interest in the investment of outside capital in the new territory. As Territorial Governor (two separate periods) he provided a blueprint for sound development and a farsighted approach to future statehood. As Delegate to the State Constitutional Convention (1838–1839), he provided legal talent, intimate knowledge, unswerving devotion in the development of the Constitution upon which admission to the Union was predicated.

But Call's story here becomes more than the story of his own life and the lives of his descendants. It becomes the story of a beautiful and strongly built house, The Grove, its tragedies and its triumphs under changing lovers and in the shadow of national and state struggles.

This, then, may be regarded in the end as the true love story of a house, a tiny star in the civilization of its time.

Tallahassee, Florida   LeRoy Collins
December 1, 1971

Acknowledgments

WITHOUT THE HELP of many others I could not have put this book together and I am deeply grateful to all who assisted in ways large and small.

Miss Dorothy Dodd, former State Librarian, has been patient and competent in reviewing my facts and script. She also helped in assessing the value of photographs and in working with the printers over details with which I had had no prior experience whatever.

Mrs. Olive Cross, professor in the English Department of Florida State University, and neighbor of ours on Dog Island, has been an interested, devoted, and knowledgeable friend. I would not have attempted the project without her confidence and encouragement.

Miss Daisy Parker, now Assistant Vice President for Academic Affairs of Florida State University, and a professor of public administration and political science, has been a treasured friend for years. She read the manuscript and made helpful suggestions.

Dr. Robert Akerman, now Dean of Kennesaw Junior College, Marietta, Georgia, formerly head of the Department of Government of Florida Southern College, Lakeland, has shared with me over many years his vast interest in and knowledge of Florida's history and politics. And so has Miss Margaret Chapman, now serving on the faculty of Queens College in North Carolina, but who until recently served with great distinction as Special Collections Librarian at the University of South Florida, Tampa.

Mr. George Ruppel, former Chairman of the County Commission of Pinellas County, and present member of the State's Pollution Control Board, has been helpful beyond measure in outmaneuvering the many pragmatic reasons which have cried "no" to the undertaking.

The following also have helped importantly and each will understand how without the need for me to supply details:

Jim Hardee, David Arnold, Frank Weaner, Jewel Crum, Ed Price, Jack Cromartie, Ruth and T. J. Roberts, Velda Brown, C. H. Coulter, Jenkie Allen, John Correll, Jo and Allen Morris, Dorothy and John D. MacDonald, Bruce Roberts, John D. Pennekamp, Bob Fokes, Thelma and R. H. Gibson, Dottie Sample, Bill Durden, Vincent Akra, Ruth Chapman, Irving Cypen, Dick Edgerton, Frank Buchanan, Nelson Poynter, Jack Daniel, Howard Friedman, David Bludworth, A. B. Byrd, Daz and Richard Harkness, George Cooper, Audrey Griscom, Jay Janis, Karl Holland, Edwin White, Verle Pope, Mary Taylor Olive, Ruth Nickerson, Howard Anderson, Bob Pittman, Ted Phelps, Richard Pettigrew, Sherwin Simmons, Ellen Whiteside, Phil Martin, John Germany, Jackson Logan, Clif Paisley, Virginia Coker, Julian V. Smith, Theodore Groom, Bob Ervin, Joe Jacobs, Rainey Cawthon, Herbert Davidson, and Sax Lloyd.

Members and the staff of Ervin, Pennington, Varn and Jacobs, my law firm in Tallahassee, have helped in checking, advising, proofreading, typing, making copies, etc.— two secretaries especially working beyond the call of duty, Mrs. Lynn Cox and Mrs. Judy Dierking. I will be everlastingly grateful to all of them.

In this work I gained a new appreciation for the Florida State Library. This is a remarkable institution. Following the past leadership of the late W. T. Cash, and Miss Dorothy Dodd, the present director Henry J. Blasick and his superb staff are not only efficient but they transmit the rare quality of seeming to find joy in helping. I don't believe there is another state agency in which the staff gives so much with such good spirit. They are cramped for room, and I am sure they don't have all they need in other respects too, but they seem totally devoted to making the most of what they have.

Finally, I express appreciation for the constant help of the members of my family. They have lived with my pluses and minuses, in the valleys and on the mountain tops, and have made themselves a vital and enduring part of it all.

1

☆ ☆ ☆ ☆ ☆

The Read-Alston Duel

POLITICAL SETTLEMENT, CIRCA 1839

THIS IS NOT the story of the ten little Indians. It is the story of five big white men. But both stories end the same way: And then there was none.

It is the incredible story of how, in Florida, during 1839–1840, three strong, honorable men allowed a false sense of honor, fueled by unbridled emotion, to impel them to kill, with resulting vicious backlashes that brought an end to them all.

Meet first the Alstons. The head of the family, Colonel R. A. Alston, had settled in Georgia. He was a very successful, wealthy, and influential farmer with three sons, Willis, Augustus, and Gideon, and two daughters. All of these sons were big men in stature, handsome and self-confident. They were known to be excellent marksmen, fearless in any kind of conflict. They knew weapons of all kinds and talked much of duels and dueling. They were accustomed to getting what they wanted—whether land, money, or women; and many of their conquests came by intimidation or through other questionable means.

Living with the Alston family in Georgia was a young, socially acceptable, suave Castilian named Pepin. Willis had picked him up in Nashville when he had visited there to pay court to a Miss Trimble. Everyone in the family seemed to be very fond of Pepin, though it was later

1

thought that Gideon had developed some friction in his feelings for him.

One evening, the three sons, their father, and Pepin were inspecting some dueling pistols of rare quality in the living room of their home. Pepin and Gideon took several of the guns outside the house to practice firing them. The others, who remained inside, heard shots from the yard but paid little attention. Soon, however, Pepin came back in and calmly announced that he had shot and killed Gideon by mistake. There were no witnesses, but enough doubt arose about Pepin's story to make it impossible for him to remain with the family. He went into the Navy and was reported, some months later, to have drowned mysteriously "in the tropical seas." All this was just a prologue.

Soon afterwards the family acquired substantial holdings of farm lands in North Florida just below the Georgia-Florida line, near the village of Miccosukee, and the father, daughters, and the two surviving sons, Willis and Augustus, moved there. They increased their wealth and were respected socially as well as politically. Willis left Florida, however, moving to Texas, only to return later on a mission of murder, the details of which are related hereafter.

Augustus became very prominent in politics in territorial and national affairs. He became the acknowledged leader of the Whig Party, which was pro-bank in the banking controversy that raged in the Jackson presidential years and on into the term of his successor, Martin Van Buren. The Democrats were determined to bring about banking reforms which they felt were badly needed, and the Whigs represented the strong conservative viewpoint in opposing such. In those days on the Florida frontier, the people were rugged and proud, and their emotions were easily set aflame by differences in political viewpoints and party alignments.

There was in Tallahassee at this time a young political

leader named Leigh Read (pronounced: Lay Reed). During the five years following 1836, his reputation rose rapidly, and for good reasons. His first political position was the lowly, but honorable, office of engrossing clerk of the Territorial Council. Here, he demonstrated a high degree of dedication and dependability in his efforts, and those with whom he worked held him in high esteem.

He had a distinguished military career, commanding the Battalion of Florida Volunteers in the Indian Campaign of 1836 with conspicuous competence and bravery. He was wounded in this service. Later, upon the recommendation of General Richard Keith Call, he was appointed by President Jackson as brigadier general in command of the First Brigade of Florida Militia. In this role, he was actively involved in field operations and was later given the assignment to head the military in the protection of the Florida frontier.

President Van Buren also appointed General Read to serve as United States marshal for the Middle District of Florida, a post he held only for the remainder of Van Buren's term as President. He was married twice, first to Miss Teresa Bellamy, daughter of a prominent Jefferson County planter, and later to Miss Eliza Branch, daughter of John Branch, a former governor of North Carolina, who was to become Florida's last territorial governor.

Read continued his interest in civil activities. He was a delegate to the convention to form a constitution for Florida in 1838–1839 and became presiding officer of the lower house of the Territorial Council. He was an ardent Democrat, very strongly aligned with his party against the banks. He was physically attractive and well liked, except by those who opposed his political views. He had excellent prospects to achieve any honor or hold any office within the gift of the people of Florida. While Read's military experience was extensive and well known, his civil pursuits seemed more suited to his personality. There was nothing about him to suggest that he would ever desire to settle political disagreements through violent means. Nor was his personality such that his enemies would especially fear him in any encounter.

At least two leading Whigs challenged him to fight a duel over heated words concerning the bank issue, but Read brushed these aside with the comment that if he had to fight a duel he would prefer to take on a more prominent Whig, such as Augustus Alston, whom he regarded as "the bulldog of the party."

Later, upon the urging of several of his Whig friends, Alston actually sent the challenge. Some felt that Read would decline and that Alston would pick up the credit for backing him down. But Read did accept, and arrangements were duly made for a "duel to the death."

Yager rifles were selected by Read and agreed upon. These were deadly weapons at close range. The barrel was short and a fair shot could hardly miss unless he became wounded by his antagonist before he had a chance to fire. The site chosen for the duel was northeast of Tallahassee, just over the Georgia State line and only a few miles from the Alston place. The entire community was deeply disturbed because most feared the duel would lead to the death of its favorite son, Read.

Augustus Alston's sisters, however, were extremely confident that their brother would be victorious, as he always had been in encounters with other men, whatever the nature of the conflict. And, too, they had absolute confidence that he was the best shot in the territory. Alston and his party were to leave their plantation home for the duel site in a carriage drawn by four horses, two white ones and two black ones. In a light hearted mood he told his sisters that they could watch from the cupola on the top of their spacious home near Lake Miccosukee for his return and that if he had been victorious the two white horses would be in the lead, but if he had lost the two black ones would lead.

The principals, their seconds, and those in charge gathered at the place agreed upon at dawn. Everyone answered the questions confirming their knowledge of the rules. The weapons were taken up and the duelists assumed their positions back to back. On the count of ten paces, each was to turn and fire at will. "One, two, three, four, five"—the paces were being taken—"nine, ten." Both men turned, but Alston, after turning discharged his weapon before he could raise it and aim. Read deliberately and carefully raised his rifle, aimed at his surprised and helpless foe, and fired. Alston fell, mortally wounded.

The sisters, with high spirited confidence, from their lofty perch, scanned the hill top from which they could get their first glimpse of the return of the conquering Augustus. They knew it would be soon but there was an ominous time drag. Then they came slowly—the black horses in the lead.

The duel and the killing of Augustus Alston did not settle anything. The fires of hatred raged with even greater bitterness. Alston's friends contended that their man fired either accidentally, due to an over-sensitive trigger, or purposefully to abort the duel, and that, had Read been a gentleman, he would have respected his foe's position, and held his fire. General Read's friends countered with the assertion that it was firmly agreed that the duel was to the death, and that Read was entirely correct in firing as he did.

Alston's sisters, ablaze now with shock and hatred for Read, extracted the lead from Alston's body and cast it into a new bullet. This they sent to their brother, Willis, in Texas with a demand that he come home and avenge their brother's "treacherous murder" by Read. They wanted Willis to use the same lead that had killed Augustus to tear open Read's heart.

It wasn't long before the community of Tallahassee and its environs heard about what the sisters had done, and rumor was running wild that Willis was on his way to Tallahassee. General Read's friends urged him to stay armed for his own protection, and this he did.

It was a gay night in Tallahassee. The Speaker's Ball was being held at Brown's Hotel. General Read had been elected to this office and was giving the traditional dinner for his friends (a tradition, incidentally, which has continued to this day). While the banquet was at its highest point of merriment, there was a commotion at the far end of the hall, from where a tall figure with hat pulled down low over his eyes and wearing a long cloak strode toward Read. There were gasps as several people exclaimed, "It's Willis Alston!" Alston then threw the cape back and flung his hat aside, revealing himself to the crowd. At this point, Read rose from his chair and reached for his gun. Alston was now bounding toward Read clutching a bowie knife. Read fired and the bullet struck Alston's hand, slightly wounding him. Alston charged Read and the two men met. Others pulled them apart, however, with the result that Read received only minor cuts and Willis was not further injured.

A month or so after Willis's attack on Read, he made careful plans for another attempt. He knew the General would walk past a certain house, so he arranged with the owner, one Michael Ledwith, to stay there. When Read and a friend strolled past. Alston waited with a double-barrel shotgun. His first shot, which was from some distance, caught Read by complete surprise and seriously wounded him. While Read was reeling from this, Alston walked up very close to him and fired the second barrel load into his head, killing him instantly.

Alston was arrested and jailed. With the help of friends, and reportedly at a cost of $30,000 paid in bribes, he later escaped and fled back to Texas, where he settled in a place called Brazoria.

After Alston had lived there for several months, a doctor by the name of Stewart received some information about the killing in Tallahassee which identified Willis Alston as a murderer. Stewart expressed great disfavor about such a vicious killer and fugitive from justice living among the

decent, law abiding citizens of little Brazoria. Willis
Alston heard about the doctor's remarks and reduced the
charges made against him to writing. The next time the
two men met each was mounted on his horse. Willis
stopped the doctor and handed to him the sheet of paper
on which the charges were written, asking that he admit
or deny that he had made such remarks. Dr. Stewart took
the paper and dismounted from his horse on the opposite
side from Willis. While thus concealed, he drew his gun,
came from around his horse, and shot Willis in the
stomach. Willis, though badly wounded grabbed his own

Leigh Read's burial place. Bradford Cemetery, nine miles north of
Tallahassee. Read, his daughter, and wife, are buried in the three
center vaults. Read's vault is inscribed: Sacred to the memory of Gen.[1]
Leigh Read, born in Sumner County, Tennessee, August 11th 1809;
died in Florida: April 27th 1841. Augustus Alston is buried in an
obscure unmarked grave eight miles eastward near his family home
site at Lake Miccosukee.

shotgun and poured a load of buckshot into Dr. Stewart, killing him instantly. Willis was arrested forthwith and placed in the local jail. Though seriously wounded, his spirits were still high and he amused himself by playing a fiddle a friend had brought him. One of his servants obtained permission to visit him in the jail and came with a rope carefully wound around his body. The servant, avoiding detection, slipped the rope to Willis to aid him in making an escape.

In the meantime, however, Dr. Stewart's friends were busy with plans of their own. They had decided that Willis was such a sinister character that he had to be dealt with outside the law. A mob stormed the little jail and took Willis outside. The *Florida Mirror* described the final act in the life and death of Willis Alston as follows:

A mob pressed through the doors, but the dauntless hero never quailed. He sat there fiddling in lordly contempt of pain and death, looking upon his inhuman assailants with unblanched face. They dragged him out, swinging him in a blanket which they knotted at the ends. There, muffled up from the light of day, but with the old fearlessness blazing in his heart and the old dauntless smile playing on his lips, his body riddled with a shower of lyncher's bullets, the last of the Alstons died. A lion-like race they were, their gentle blood flaming into passion at the slightest insult—generous of life and gold alike—fitter in their imperious habits and princely ways for the days of chivalry and realm of barons than for our prosaic days and our commonplace land.

2

☆ ☆ ☆ ☆ ☆

Hell Off Hatteras

THE TROPICAL HURRICANE was wild, strong and long lasting. She was born somewhere in the Caribbean in the early days of October 1837, and the first record of her willful intent to be violent and hurtful came when out of the east she lashed across the southern tip of Florida, and whirled on westward into the Gulf of Mexico. There she turned sharply northward, and then easterly, leaving the Gulf in a state of violent commotion as she banged into Northwest Florida. On October 7, she moved toward the North Atlantic with still strong winds. In those days winds were not measured; neither was a hurricane's position and direction of movement communicated to the world.

On the morning of this same day, with wind and water calm and the sky clear, the steamship *Home* pulled away from its dock on East River, New York City, with Charleston, South Carolina, as her destination. Neither her crew nor passengers had any reason to suspect the awful fate which lay ahead. A sparkling new ship, this being only her third voyage, she carried a crew of forty, including her officers, and 130 passengers. On the day before, the *New York Daily Express* had printed an editorial complimenting the ship and her owners for providing such a fine opportunity to make a run by sea from New York to Charleston in sixty-four hours, incredibly fast for that day. Doubtless this rather unusual publicity influenced some passengers to book passage in the last hours before sailing.

The *Home* was not seaworthy, however, regardless of the

favorable impressions. With no warning she moved into the ominous wind and waves of the northeast-bound hurricane just south of Cape Hatteras some fifty hours after sailing. The blackened seas mounted rapidly, and the *Home* lost her steerageway. Unable to hold a heading, her cargo loose in her holds, she banged violently about and the bulkheads collapsed from progressive flooding. The terror-stricken passengers were overcome by the helplessness of the ship in the accelerating fury, and ninety of them and the crew perished in the rage.

If such a catastrophe should happen now, the world would be made aware of it in minutes. In that year of 1837, it was nearly a week before the news got to Charleston, only 200 miles away.

In the churchyard of St. John's Episcopal of Tallahassee, near the front entrance on the right as one enters, stands a marble obelisk, darkly streaked with age. Inscribed upon it is this memorial:

SACRED TO THE MEMORY OF
HARDY BRYAN CROOM

Born in North Carolina
October 8, 1797

Died near Cape Hatteras
October 9, 1837

Amiable without weakness, learned without arrogance, wealthy without ostentation, and benevolent without parade. He sought not the world's admiration, but noiselessly pursued his path through life, finding his purest earthly pleasure in the bosom of his family, the society of his friends and the companionship of his books. The best tribute to his worth is to be found in the affectionate remembrance of those, who having known him from boyhood, loved him while living, and deplored him dead. This marble seeks also to preserve the remembrance of

FRANCES H. CROOM,
Wife of Hardy B. Croom,
and of their children,

HENRIETTA MARY CROOM,
aged 15 years,

WILLIAM HENRY CROOM,
aged 10 years,

JUSTINA ROSA CROOM,
aged 7 years,

all of whom perished with the unfortunate husband and father in the wreck of their steamboat "Home" on the night of the 9th of October, 1837.

Though the bodies of none of the Croom family that were recovered were buried in Tallahassee or in Florida, and though there were legal questions raised as to Mr. Croom's state of domicile at the time of his death, I have always felt that is was appropriate that St. John's would thus manifest its care for this family and its sorrow over the stark tragedy that took their lives.

The Crooms were a very remarkable family, not only the ones who died in the wreck of the *Home,* but the others. Their growing relationship with Florida in those early pioneer years was constructive and important. They were the kind of rich, proud, aristocratic people who felt an obligation to make their lives and resources important to the general welfare as well as to themselves. Their homes were large and hospitable with the libraries perhaps the best equipped, and most used, rooms.

General William Croom, who died in 1829 had his family base in Lenoir County, North Carolina. He had developed several plantations in that area and was by all standards an affluent and respected citizen. His first wife, Mary Bryan, was also from an influential and politically active family of North Carolina. They had four children: Hardy Bryan Croom (who was lost on the *Home*), Susan Matilda Croom, Bryan Croom (not to be confused with Hardy Bryan), and Richard Croom.

From a second marriage to Elizabeth Whitfield there were five other children, including another son, George Alexander Croom.

General William Croom, in the mid 1820s, had started the family's migration southward to Florida through the purchase of farming lands in Gadsden County in West Florida. His three sons, Bryan, Richard and, later, George, all followed and became citizens of Florida; but the General never moved his citizenship from North Carolina nor did Hardy Bryan Croom though he had vast interests in Florida. He and his family spent much of their time here, and it is conceded that he was in act of moving his domicile when he lost his life.

In Florida, while the Crooms' plantation holdings were firmly established in Jackson and Gadsden Counties, the home pattern strongly tended toward Tallahassee, the territorial capital, where many of their descendants now live. Bryan Croom, who in the late 1820s established his home in Gadsden County which he named Rocky Comfort, later built Goodwood in Leon County near Tallahassee. Goodwood, one of Florida's finest antebellum houses, was acquired by the late State Senator William C. Hodges of Tallahassee and continues to be occupied by his widow, the present Mrs. Margaret Hood and her husband, Col. Thomas M. Hood.

Hardy Bryan Croom was born in 1797 on the North Carolina family base. He was graduated from the University of North Carolina and later received a Masters Degree. Inheriting a fortune from his father's estate, he became primarily interested in pursuing his studies in many fields including geology, mineralogy and botany. He authored many articles on plants, developing a special interest in the flora of Florida. His first holdings were along the banks of the Apalachicola River in West Florida. Here he discovered a species of tree which is found only in very limited localities in but few areas of the world. He gave to this tree the name *Torreya* taxifolia, honoring Dr. John Torrey, a famous botanist of that time who lived in New York. The State of Florida in more recent years has given the Torreya tree considerable attention. A state park on the banks of the Apalachicola where it still thrives is named for it. Also, a handsome specimen now grows on the State Capitol grounds.

Hardy Bryan Croom was accepted into the membership of many prominent national scientific societies because of his contributions in research and had authored a botanical catalog which was being printed at the time of his death. The publication was under the direction of Dr. Torrey who makes the following statement in the preface:

> Mr. Croom was an ardent lover of botany. . . . In his annual visits to Florida he availed himself of the opportunity which he enjoyed of examining the vegetable productions of the interesting regions through which he passed. His earlier botanical papers are inserted in the American Journal of Science. . . .
>
> Among the new plants discovered by Mr. Croom and communicated to me, are a beautiful evergreen Andromeda; an arborescent Taxus, allied to T canadensis, but attaining a height of thirty feet; a noble new genus of coniferae with the foliage of Taxus and a fruit as large as a nutmeg, which Dr. Arnott will shortly publish under the name of Torreya; and a very distinct new genus, to which I have given the name Croomia, in honor of my departed friend.

In 1834 Hardy Bryan Croom purchased and began the development of a plantation in Leon County. He stated at the time that he was impressed with the location for his future family home because of its closeness to Tallahassee with its good society, and the rich quality of the rolling hill lands which bordered upon beautiful Lake Lafayette. From 1830 until his death he had brought his family to Tallahassee for large portions of every year, and the new permanent living plan he had decided upon was to establish a summer residence in Charleston and move his family on to Florida. The steamboat *Home* was to take him on the first leg of the journey. Tragically, it became the last.

DARK AGONY

As the sullen sea rose and fell and the *Home* was called

upon to scale higher and higher crests and sink into lower and lower troughs, approaching a point off Cape Hatteras, the Captain knew that he was in a position of danger that would likely become worse before it got better. He considered the possibility of heading farther seaward to minimize the chances of running aground, but this would mean hazarding being farther from help from other vessels if needed, plus a loss of navigation position fixing. The other choice was to move as close inland as depth and visibility would permit and hopefully find a lee. This would have obvious advantages if he could keep his ship from becoming awash by the sea breaking over her in the shallower water causing an almost certain flooding of the engine room with a resulting loss of all power.

Right or wrong, he decided on the latter course though his soundings indicated there was little draft margin to permit moving much closer toward the shore. And soon the swells had the decks awash and the ship was rolling precipitously in the black seaway. The crew and passengers alike frantically were scooping with buckets trying desperately to keep the water as low in the engine room as possible. The first suggestion of engine failure came with spasmodic interruptions of the rhythmic strokes of the steam engine . . . speeding up when both side wheels were clear of the water, then laboring slower when deeply submerged. The situation became worse when operating pressure began to drop because of the uncontrollable water levels in the boiler caused by the violent rolling.

The fate of the *Home* became sealed when the rate of flooding exceeded the valiant efforts of those manning the pumps, buckets, anything they could put their hands on. As the propulsion system failed further, the night was punctuated with cries of pain from the scalding steam on human flesh, mingled with the shouts, moaning and gibbering of the terrified victims.

The boiler fires were extinguished in the progressive flooding and this meant the *Home* was out of control and her doom was sealed as, helpless, she yielded herself to the fury of wind and sea. As a last resort, efforts were made to hoist a sail that might help to drive the ship on the shore south of the Cape. This would have provided a better chance for the survival of all those on board, but the heaving and lurching with the shrieking wind, plus the loss of freeboard made existence top side impossible. A Mr. B. B. Hussey, one of the surviving passengers, a few days later wrote this account:

> At about eleven o'clock, those who had been employed in bailing were compelled to leave the cabin, as the boat had sunk until the deck was nearly level with the water; and it appeared ... that all would soon be swallowed up by the foaming waves. The heaving of the lead indicated an approach to the shore. Soon was the cheering intelligence of 'Land, Land,' announced by those on the lookout. This, for a moment, aroused the sinking energies of all, when a general bustle ensued in the hasty, but trifling preparations that could be made for safety, as soon as the boat should strike. But what were the feelings of an anxious multitude, when, instead of land, a range of angry breakers were visible just ahead; and land, if it could be seen at all, was but half perceptible in the distance far beyond.... The boat, at length, strikes,—it stops—as motionless as a bar of lead. A momentary pause follows,—as if the angel of death shrank from so dreadful a work of slaughter. But soon the work of destruction commenced. A breaker, with a deafening crash, swept over the boat, carrying its unfortunate victims into the deep. At the same time, a simultaneous rush was made toward the bow of the boat. The forward deck was covered. Another breaker came, with irresistible force,— and all within its sweep disappeared. Our numbers were now frightfully reduced. The roaring of the waters, together with the dreadful crash of breaking timbers, surpasses the power of description. Some of the remaining passengers sought shelter from the encroaching dangers, by retreating to the passage, on the lee side of the boat, that leads from the after to the forward deck, as if to be as far as possible from the grasp of death.

Another eyewitness account was given by Mr. Vanderzee, another surviving passenger. It was printed in the *Southern Patriot,* a daily newspaper published in Charleston, as follows:

> The ladies had all been requested to forward, as the place where they were more likely to reach the shore, being nearest the beach, but a heavy sea struck her there, and swept nearly one-half of them into the sea, and they were drowned. One boat was stove at this time. Another small boat was launched, with two or three persons in it, but capsized. The long boat was then put overboard, filled with persons, 25 in number, it is supposed, but did not get 15 feet from the side of the steamer before she upset, and it is the belief of our informant that not one of the individuals in her ever reached the shore. The sea was breaking over the boat at this time with tremendous force, and pieces of her were breaking off at times, and floating toward the shore, on some of which persons were clinging. One lady, with a child in her arms, was in the act of mounting the stairs to the upper deck, when the smoke stack fell, and doubtless killed her and her child on the spot. Some few of the ladies were lashed to the boat. Mrs. Schroeder was confined in this manner to one of the braces of the boat, and another lady was tied to the same piece of timber. Mr. Vanderzee was standing near them, when the latter lady slipped along the brace so that the water broke over her. Mr. V. seized her by the clothes and held her up for some time, and made every exertion that was possible to release her, but failed; She herself endeavored to unloose the rope, but was unable to do so, and shortly afterwards the brace broke off from the boat, and went towards the shore; Mrs. Schroeder still fastened to it, while her unfortunate companion slipped off and was lost. Mr. S. after striking the beach, with great presence of mind, drew the timber up on the beach so far as to prevent it from being washed away by the waves, and was thus saved."

There are doubtless many poignant stories in each life that was ended that awful night. Every casualty was more than a statistic. No one has followed up an investigation of who each was, what his life had been, what it might have become. These records have been largely locked up in the hearts and minds of those who cared.

The late Honorable Dan Redfearn, distinguished lawyer of the Miami Bar has done a splendid job in uncovering many of the facts regarding this trag-

THE LAW SUIT

Interesting litigation in Leon County, Florida, followed the sinking of the *Home* and the death of the Hardy Bryan Croom family. None of these victims left a will, and in dispute were (1) the underlying issue of in which state, North Carolina or Florida was the family domiciled at the time of death; and then (2) who was the last survivor, the father, the mother or one of the children. The personal estate of the father was by far the most valuable and if the father was the last of the family to die, then all his estate would go to his brothers and sisters no matter in which of the two states he was found to be domiciled. If the mother was the last survivor, then she would have inherited the estates of her husband and children, and upon her death her relatives would have inherited from her. If, however, one of the children had been the last survivor and North Carolina was the state of domicile, then the personal estate would go to the maternal next of kin, as provided under the laws of that state; but if Florida was the state of domicile, under its laws the estate would be distributed between the maternal *and* paternal next of kin.

The suit was filed in January of 1839 by the maternal heirs of the Croom children against the sister and brothers of Hardy Bryan Croom. The brother, Bryan Croom, who claimed in his own right and as the purchaser and successor in interest to whatever his sister and two brothers were entitled, actually carried the burden of the defense. More particularly the plaintiffs claimed that North Carolina was the state of domicile, and that the boy, William Henry Croom, was the last to die. If so, then he had inherited from his father prior to his own death, and under North Carolina laws his personal estate passed to the plaintiffs.

edy as it related to the Croom family. His article, "The Steamship Home," has been published on three occasions in the *Florida Law Journal*. First in the May 1935 issue, a revision in November 1947 issue, and the last in the February 1963 issue. I have utilized much of the results of Mr. Redfearn's research in this piece.

Against this claim, the defendant contended that Hardy Bryan Croom had left North Carolina with the firm intention of making his domicile in Florida and that the family domicile at the time of their death was in Florida; that the father had survived his wife and all his children, and that upon his death all the estate passed to his sister and brothers.

Hardy Bryan Croom's children were all rather extraordinary. Henrietta was described by the New York *Daily Express* in its issue of October 26, 1837 in these terms:

> Miss Henrietta Croom was sixteen years of age, a young lady of great personal charm and accomplishments, and very beautiful. She was a native of North Carolina and had been about three years in this city, where she had acquired an excellent education at the boarding school of Madame Chegaray. By her agreeable deportment and sweetness of manner, she had formed for herself an admiring host of ardent friends.

The little girl Justina Rosa (7) was vivacious, charming and adored by all of her family.

William Henry (10) was exceptionally intelligent and talented. He had spent the winters of 1831, 1832, 1833 and 1834 in Florida and attended school in Gadsden County near his uncle Bryan's home, Rocky Comfort. Later he was enrolled in school in New York. Here was the likely beginnings of a man of great stature, perhaps very much in the mold of his father.

The father, Hardy Bryan Croom, was not regarded as being in the best of health, but this was thought to be due to a generally weak physical condition, and the erosion of the most common illnesses that most people in the South were called upon to endure in those days.

Much testimony was taken by the trial court to shed all possible light on just what happened in the case of each of the Croom family on that fateful night. The State Supreme Court in its review found that when the *Home* became grounded and thus hopelessly wrecked, many passengers were crowding the gangway to abandon ship. Mr. Croom was remembered as being there with his wife and her aunt, each clutching to one of his arms. The little daughter, Justina, was in front of these three and the boy William Henry was behind. At this moment a great breaker swept through the gangway and when it had passed over only two of the group were left, Mr. Croom and the boy. Thus, it was thought that Mrs. Croom and Justina were the first two of the family to die.

One witness remembered clearly a scene when just before the grounding many of the passengers were still trying their best to pump and bail water out to keep the engine fires from being extinguished. He saw Mr. Croom with a lady on each arm and behind him was "the little boy whose voice he recognized as the son of Mr. Croom, who was crying and calling to his father to save him."

Then there was the testimony of a Mr. Conrad Quinn that:

> Mr. Croom stood on the leeside near the cabin door as you go out; his family were in that cabin on deck; heard the son ask the father to swim with him; Mr. Croom was taken off with the sea at the time the breakers were washing away the cabin; witness went to leeward side of the boat and got on wheel-house; about a dozen were on the forecastle, the Captain among them; most of the passengers were there. While witness was on the wheel-house a young lady came up, who was Miss [Henrietta] Croom; she came on to wheel-house and held on to same piece of timber witness did, and stood there about five minutes; she was washed off with the wheel-house.

Henrietta thus was assumed to have been lost, but apparently Mr. Croom and William Henry were still surviving. Verifying this was the statement of a Mr. Bishop:

> ... when the boat struck, he saw a dozen ladies, and some few gentlemen come out of the cabin door on deck; they were all swept off by the breakers; saw a number in the sea; Mr. Croom could not have been swept off then; saw him afterwards. Witness found no one in the afterpart but

himself; thinks the others were swept off into the sea; after this he saw Mr. Croom and his son against kitchen door; never saw Mr. Croom afterwards, and should say, from the circumstances, that he was taken off by the sea before the boat went to pieces; before the breaker passed he saw the two, and after it passed saw the boy alone, and never saw Mr. Croom afterwards; did not see any other of the family after he missed Mr. Croom; the stern went to pieces first, the fore part next, the middle last; the gallows frame was the last that fell, and the same breaker took off the wheel-house; the next took the portion where witness stood, which was the leeward side and a portion near the wheel; the last I saw perish was Master Croom; witness and young Croom were on the part of the wreck on which they floated before it parted.

Mr. Bishop later also added:

I saw him [William Henry] floating out to sea, seemingly upright, with his face towards the part of the wreck from which he had just been carried, and distinctly heard the water in his throat, as if strangling. This was the last I saw of him. When the next breaker came I went ashore on it.

So the evidence would indicate that William Henry was the last of the family to perish.

I agree with Mr. Redfearn in his moving tribute to young William Henry Croom:

One cannot help admiring the fight this ten-year-old boy, William Henry Croom, made for his life. The evidence shows that, while the father was living, the little boy was crying and calling to his father to save him, but that after his father was washed overboard the boy, despite the raging waves and the darkness of the night, reached a floating piece of the wreck on which there were four men, Bishop, Cady, Johnson, and Vanderzee. He held on for 30 to 45 minutes until the piece of the wreck was grounded near the shore, when he was jarred off, or swept off by the return of the water from a heavy wave, or breaker.

The trial court found for the defendant, the brother Bryan Croom, and ordered the suit dismissed.* An appeal

*Mr. Redfearn in describing the state of the law confronting the court points to many presumptions which existed under the civil, or Roman law.

was taken to the Supreme Court of Florida and after having the case for many long years, the court in 1857 reversed the lower court holding that in this calamity in which all of the family perished, Hardy Bryan Croom survived his wife and his daughter, Justina; that the daughter Henrietta survived her father and that William Henry survived his sister Henrietta, and thus was the last surviving member of the family. The domicile of the family was held to be in North Carolina. Under this ruling the maternal grandmother in North Carolina received all the personal estate (which was most of it). The real estate in Florida (the descent and distribution being controlled by Florida laws) was divided between maternal and paternal heirs (¼ to the former and ¾ to the latter).

The legal principle approved by the Florida Supreme Court was that:

> In a question of survivorship, arising out of a common calamity, the legal presumption founded upon the circumstances of age, size, or physical strength, does not obtain in our jurisprudence. It is a doctrine of the civil law.

> But when the calamity, though common to all, consists of a series of successive events, separated from each other in point of time and character, and each likely to produce death upon the several victims according to the degree of exposure to it, in such case the difference of age, sex and physical strength becomes a matter of evidence and may be considered.

This continued to be the law of Florida until 1933 when it was established by statute that:

For example, under these rules if members of a family died in a common disaster and all were 60 or over, the youngest was presumed to have survived. If all were under 15 then the eldest was presumed to have outlived the others. As between sexes, males were presumed to outlive females. The Code of Napoleon of France included very similar provisions. The common law of England, which had been adopted as the law of Florida by the Legislative Council of the Territory of Florida, did not indulge any such presumptions. Under the common law, if two or more persons died in a common disaster and if evidence could not be produced to prove which died first, there was no presumption, and for estate administration purpose each estate would be administered as if each decedent survived the other.

Where there is no clear and convincing evidence of the order in which the death of two or more persons occurred, no one of such persons shall be presumed to have died first, and the estate of each shall pass as though he had survived the other or others. F.S.A. 731.26 (27).

This statute has been further implemented by other legislation subsequently and it is the writer's opinion that if a situation similiar to the wreck of the *Home* were to occur now, and the estate should be administered under the jurisdiction of Florida courts, it would be held that the evidence of survivorship did not meet the rule of being "clear and convincing," and the estate would be administered as though each decedent survived the others.

Fortunately, such a calamity is not likely to recur. Ships are built better, navigation aids are better, weather reporting and hurricane tracking are better, communications are better, safety requirements are much stronger. For example, there were only two life preservers on board the *Home,* and they were privately owned. The *Home* disaster contributed strongly to a public demand that resulted in much mandatory legislation by Congress which vastly improved the safety of transportation by water.

ASEOLA.
A SEMINOLE LEADER.

3

☆ ☆ ☆ ☆ ☆

Osceola

FLORIDA'S NUMBER ONE ALL-TIME MILITANT

THE HERO OF this story is a Seminole Indian named "Asi Yahola," which is derived from the Indian words, "Asi," and "Yahola." "Asi" was the word for a drink that was black in color and bad in taste. At the Green Corn Dance, when the golden ears were ripe in June, each brave swallowed a gourdful of this ceremonial black drink. As the brave finished, he and the other warriors gave a loud cry: "Yahola!"

The English adaptation, "Osceola," came into common usage as the Indian became known to English-speaking people, and he will be referred to here by that name.

Osceola was neither from original Seminole stock—the early Alachua Indians—nor from the Creeks who later migrated to North Florida. He was descended from the hostile "Red Stick" Creeks who were routed from areas farther north in the early 1800s and came south to seek sanctuary and sustenance on land owned and controlled by Spain. The "Red Sticks" got this name from a Creek custom that called for erecting a red stick or pole in the center of a village to signify a declaration of war. It was their disposition to keep it up most of the time.

Contrary to some expressed views, this writer agrees with those who believe that Osceola was a full-blooded Indian and not a descendant of Indian and white parentage. In his mature years, most white people thought him to be one-half or one-fourth white. He was a highly-emotional and sentimental person, and it is natural that this reflection upon his parentage would set aflame strong feelings of resentment on his part.*

GROWING UP

The wise old man, Milakee, counseled him and taught him the ways of life as he understood them from experience and from his communications with the Great Spirit.

Osceola was impressed with the softness of his voice and the bright sparkle in the dark eyes, which were never more than half open. But, most of all, he was impressed with the craggy brown furrows that gave to his face character, the grace of ages, and peace; that gave to his hands a harmony with nature, like still strong bark protecting ancient tree limbs. His body was straight and his stride was strong and easy as he walked. As he sat, though relaxed, if the need came suddenly he could spring to instant action.

Milakee had a special whistle for Osceola—a slight variation from the night call of the bird, normally "purp-pur-rib." The difference was in the emphasis. As they called each other, more emphasis came on the last sound and the call became "purp-pur-*reeb*." This was still another bond that held them close together. Osceola loved this man who singled him out for so much attention and who satisfied his young hunger to know and to understand everything about his people—their sufferings, their beliefs, their hopes for the future.

Living now in the northern part of Florida, Osceola

* The writer has sought to keep the important historic facts accurate, though not complete. The events of the war, as related, are obviously very abbreviated. Also, many historians have differed widely as to various events. This is understandable—especially when one takes into account that Osceola likely could not speak English and all that has been reported from his statements has come through interpreters of the time who were mostly illiterate blacks. But it is not the purpose of this piece to educate. Details have been chronicled by better-informed and more able writers. Primarily, it is sought here to stimulate renewed interest in, and understanding for, Florida's foremost militant of all time in the cause of human rights.

came to understand more clearly why his mother, after being abandoned by his father, fled with him south when pressured to move west to lands now embraced in Arkansas and Oklahoma, where Indians were being herded into reservations. He learned about black people who had escaped from being the slaves of the white settlers. Large numbers of them had found refuge with the Seminoles of North Florida. Osceola learned to feel a deep sense of care and responsibility for these black people, just as he felt for his own people. As Milakee had explained it, the Great Spirit had made people of different colors and different ways of life. He had given to all people the use of land, trees, plants, water and wildlife. There were no differences in people in their relation to these things, or to each other. But when people became greedy and sought to injure and destroy other people, or to take more than their share of what had been given to all, then the Great Spirit became angry and expected those who were injured to strike down the offenders.

As Osceola grew into his teens, he became the strongest and most skillful of all the youths of his village. Though average in physical size and raw strength, he was greatly admired by his people, Indians and Blacks, because he was a fierce and brave competitor who usually was the victor in whatever the situation that challenged him.

This was all a part of Milakee's plan for making a war chief, though Osceola did not know this. The old man often made arrangements for trips the two of them would make.

Once, on a full moon, they journeyed together overnight to the Big Spring. It was not a hard journey and the old man knew the way well: They started at nightfall, and as the two traveled, occasionally the old man would disappear and Osceola would keep on the trail alone. When Milakee rejoined him an hour or so later, he would test the boy's ability to detect his approach. The two would talk of the wild creatures of the forest, their growth and

life habits, and Osceola learned how all living things were
a part of the Great Spirit's plan.

When they drew close to the Big Spring, Osceola heard
the soft gurgle of the river. "You said we were coming to
the Big Spring, the sound is one of a running river."

"The spring is the mother of the river. We go up the
river a short distance to the Big Spring," replied the old
man.

They found the dug-out cypress which had been left
in a back water, and using his pole expertly, Milakee
moved it out into the river, which now seemed deep and
strong. As they headed upstream, the full moon was almost straight overhead, giving a bright, special sheen to
every thing—the hanging moss on the cypress tree flaring
out at the water's edge, the lily pads holding huge drops
of water that would run off like pearls when balance was
disturbed. Birds ejected from mysterious places and
screeched their resentment over the intrusion. An alligator
showed his long, furrowed head as he moved on his silent
patrol. The frogs and locusts were tuning up for their
nighttime symphony.

Osceola could see the river end just ahead. There was
a wide round space of water, lined with trees. In a moment, the old man stopped his poling and told Osceola to
look down. In the bright moonlight Osceola could see
down, down, down, as they passed over the rim and outer
walls of the giant underwater bowl. Osceola had the sensation of being suspended in the air and his hands
clenched the side of the dug-out harder and harder. But
when his fear subsided, he could see that on the bottom
there were boulders and big dark places. Milakee explained that this was where the water was coming up from.
"So much is coming up that makes the whole river that
runs to the big sea," he whispered. On the bottom, Osceola
could also see stones and objects that glistened and flashed,
reflecting the rays of the moon. Many large fish of different
kinds moved around, unmindful of being watched from
above.

On the way back to return the dug-out Milakee explained to the boy that the Great Spirit gave the spring for a supply of water and the river took the water to where it was needed. "But it is not just for us," he said. "It is for all the other things of life that need water too. The trees, the birds, the fish, the flowers, the frogs, the snakes and insects. The Great Spirit expects all men to understand that the Big Spring is to share, not to destroy, nor to deprive other people or wild creatures of its use. The same is true of land and forests." He paused, then continued, "Remember, when the white man makes slaves of the black man, he takes something which is not his to take, he takes the black man's labor, his dignity, his pride. These things belong only to the black man himself and to the Great Spirit. When the white man takes our land, he is taking something that is not his. It, too, belongs to us and to the Great Spirit. When the white man violates the Great Spirit's laws, he must be resisted."

The boy was practical. "Yes, but how?" he asked. "Doesn't the white man have more guns, more warriors, more horses?"

"Yes," Milakee said, "but you must find the answer to that question. It is for me to help you to want to be a good leader for our people. I will tell you some day of the panther and the bear."

Osceola remembered not only this trip, but many others with his counselor. They went to the sea shore once. Milakee explained to him the Great Spirit's plan of tidal rise and fall; of life in the sea and on the shore. He told him how the great sea was a purifier as well as a provider of food. On the beach, he showed him a low mound of sand and explained that underneath was where the great sea turtle, much bigger than a man, sixty days before had dug a hole and laid her eggs, over a hundred in number, covering them with sand. She had come from the sea for this function, and, having performed it, had returned, never to see her young. According to the Great Spirit's plan, this was the night the hatching-out would take place.

And that night after supper the two had come back to the place and, sitting on a sand dune nearby, overlooking the beach, they commenced their vigil. About midnight, they saw the mound tremble, then crack open, and out waddled a stream of newborn turtles. No matter in what direction they started, each soon turned toward the sound of the sea, headed for it, and swam away. "The Great Spirit has a time plan," the old man said, "for you, just as he has for the turtles. A time for you also to move out from your nest."

When they were going back home, there was a chill in the air and a flight of geese moved in toward the still warm salt marshland nearby, honking continuously to announce their arrival. Osceola asked, "Why do the big birds come each cold season, then leave when it becomes warm?"

Milakee explained that this, too, was a part of the Great Spirit's plan. They go back where it is cold to nest and hatch their young. They do not do this here, perhaps because there would be more danger to their nests and eggs here.

"How do they know where to go, how to fly on a true course?" asked Osceola.

"Only the Great Spirit knows about that," Milakee said, "but have you noticed that they fly in a formation?"

"Yes, always," Osceola replied.

"Well, there is one goose up front that leads. He is chosen by the others to point the way and keep them straight on course. Indians need leaders too. There must be someone who can see what all the Indians should do, who can convince them that he is right, and who will lead them with courage. Such a person often comes out of dark and unexpected places, but his star shines and his people look to him."

"But many feel that they are leaders," said Osceola. "How can the people tell who is the right one?"

"There are many ways," Milakee replied, "but the best test of all is that a good leader makes decisions and acts on them, while most would-be leaders just have opinions and talk about them. And the good leader's decisions are for the good of his people, not for the good of himself."

These things, too, Osceola remembered and thought about again and again.

A year or so after the beach trip, Osceola, one evening, was sitting in on a red-wheel campfire meeting, participated in by the older members of his village. For reasons that were never made clear to him, he was permitted to attend meetings like this when others his age were regarded as too young. The red wheel was formed by a group of logs with their ends brought together as at a hub and extending out as spokes in a wheel. At the center, a large fire would be laid and this would be fueled by the logs ends so that its embers would glow and keep the participants, who would sit straddling each log, warm for long hours. The village animals that ran loose would often locate themselves between the logs, out toward the perimeter. Meetings like this ended at no set time. When a participant wished to leave for any reason, he would just say goodnight and quietly depart.

On this night, it was late and all had left except Milakee and Osceola. They reviewed some of the subjects previously discussed; then Osceola asked the old man this question: "If a leader gives everything in his cause and yet cannot succeed, what does he do?"

Milakee pondered and then said: "A leader's first responsibility is not that he be successful, but that he be faithful. I want to tell you now the story of my experience with the panther and the bear." And this was Milakee's story:

> Once, in the deep woods where the ground is soft and wet, where the big trees grow, and where the vines and underbrush are so thick only the strong and wary can get through, he picked up the trail of a medium-sized panther in the soft sand of a creek bed. The panther makes a strange track easily recognized. The track shows no extensions for claws since these are retracted while walking.

There is just the pad with a round even edge. It was a female, and when he caught up with her she was making a lair for her kittens soon to come. She had chosen a place where an old tree had fallen, leaving its dirt-matted structure extending high above the ground, forming a natural backshield. She had carefully dug out and smoothed a place in the hole where the roots had been pulled up when the tree fell. There was other concealing vegetation on the other side of the hole, thus surrounding the lair and hiding it well, but leaving an opening to enter in front of the root back-barrier.

Some time later, he went back there and two kittens had been born. He guessed their age to be just under two moons. The mother was away hunting food, and he waited, hidden, to watch her return.

She came soon, bearing a large piece of a deer she had killed, and he watched her eat and feed her young. The kittens had scrambled out of the lair when they knew their mother was outside and when the meal was over they went back inside.

As he was leaving, he noticed that a colony of bees was starting to make honey in a hollow tree nearby, but this was only of passing interest at the time.

Two moons later, while near the place, he saw from tracks that a big black bear had passed, moving in the direction of the panther's lair. He followed and soon discovered that the bear was not far ahead. From his tracks, he knew he was one of the biggest bears in the forest and he wondered about the kittens.

Bears don't often attack and eat animals, but sometimes they do—and the kittens, he knew, would be tempting prey if discovered unprotected. Then he was relieved when he remembered the bees and their honey which bears usually like much better than the meat of animals. He hoped the big bear was heading for the bee tree.

When he came close to the lair, he heard the terrified scream of the kittens, and hurrying, he saw ahead the bear was beating with his huge forepaws into the lair. One kitten was dead when the bear became aware of the Indian's presence. Taking the small carcass in his mouth, the bear lurched off into the woods. The other kitten had only been bruised.

He remained concealed until the mother panther came back. She had smelled the bear and glided in, her long, golden body tensed for the fight she hoped would protect her young. Then she saw the mess the bear had made of her lair and the one remaining kitten, she sensed the other had been killed or taken off. She sensed, too, that the bear would come back soon for the kitten he had left and that now only she could save it.

The panther seemed to understand that she could not match her 120 pounds against the 600 pounds of the bear. She knew the strength of the bear's forepaws, with their powerful, sharp claws, was deadly; that they could keep her from getting close enough to get to his throat, and that if she met him in head-on combat he could slap and tear her to pieces before she could possibly get her teeth into any part of him. She knew, too, that she had to come from his back, undetected, and with such force that she could make the first strike a crippling one.

There was a limb almost as large as her body that extended over and in front of the lair about ten feet from the ground. It was strong enough and there were some concealing leaves, but the panther realized that she would have to crouch tightly against it and not make the slightest move or sound. To leap from behind the bear without moving, she could not watch him as he approached. She could see him only after he had passed under her. It would be essential, too, that the bear approach the lair from the front and move forward directly under the limb where she would be lying.

The panther turned round and round nervously, flexing her leg muscles and testing her strength by pressing her feet hard against the earth. Then, with one graceful leap, she reached the base of the limb at the tree's trunk. Here, she paused cautiously, resurveying the scene—the bear's expected point of arrival, the lair, the limb. Then she carefully moved out on the limb. Her weight caused some movement of the outer branches, but this did not discourage her. She extended her body flat against the limb and pulled her haunches forward slightly, fixing her hind claws into the limb securely.

As the panther had anticipated, the bear was now coming back to get the other kitten. They could both hear him very clearly now. The panther made her last preparation; she placed her head snugly against the limb on the side nearest the lair and away from the bear's expected approach. There was no other movement from the limb. The bear moved into the small clearing leading to the lair and standing upright looked around warily, as if he sensed that something was wrong. The panther could not see him, but she knew he was there. If he came straight to the lair to make his kill, he was in perfect line to pass under the upturned limb with the golden hump rigidly fixed above. Without looking upward, he came down on his all-fours and moved for his prey in the lair. The scent of the kitten's blood and the hunger for more food pulled him forward. One yellow eye—the one not against the limb—of the cat was the only thing that moved. It moved easily from side to side for caution, then settled down on the spot to which the bear was expected to come. When the bear was directly underneath and the panther could see the top of his head, she slightly tightened and tested her hind-claw setting, and the hair on the great cat's back rose from the slight twitching of the skin over her spine.

At this moment, the bear stopped his forward movement. He rose full length on his hind legs to make a final inspection of the area before making his second kill, and the top of his head was no more than three feet from where the panther lay. He was just three steps from the lair. One more step forward and the panther would have the angle she most desired for her leap.

Slowly, the bear turned his head from side to side, then, seeing no reason for fear, he came down slowly on his all-fours. Three more steps and the second kitten would be his for the taking. He took one, his head extended for his prey, his mouth open in anticipation.

With all the force of her weight and the lightning-fast stretch of her muscles against the secure brace of the limb, the cat leaped downward. Her mouth was opened wide and dead on target. As she struck the back of the bear's neck, the mighty jaws of the cat closed, ripping flesh and crunching bones. The bear and the panther went over together, the bear clawing at the air in a frenzy, trying in vain to reach his foe. But the grip of the panther's jaws was locked, and with every turn of the big bear's body the cat held and kept her position outside the range of those claws.

After a few moments, the panther sensed some weakening of the bear's control of his front legs and knew now that a kill could be assured if she could get to his throat to finish her job. But the claws were moving with jerks

and clumsy motions which were still deadly. The bear, perhaps, now by sheer instinct alone, was trying with his greater weight to scrape the cat from his back by rolling over her. The neck wound was gushing blood now and the panther was unable to keep it from her eyes without loosening her grip and this she dared not do.

Quite suddenly, the bear's front paws slackened and fell limp. Acting in an instant, the panther released her viselock in the back of the bear's neck and in a movement, quick and powerful, drove for his throat. As she fixed her teeth quickly and deeply into the bear's soft under-neck, she was confident that she would make her kill. Now, her belly was against that of the bear's huge chest. Her body was soaked by blood, but it wasn't hers. The bear's front paws were flopping out of control across her back and shoulders. Those forearm claws she had feared so much could no longer harm her.

In this moment of the panther's triumph, the big bear suddenly pulled his hind legs up to his chest, keeping the claws retracted. The panther considered this a part of his death spasm. But then the cat felt a stiffening of the bear's strength. She couldn't turn loose her grip on his throat, and lying there against his underside she felt the claws of those hind feet enter her tired belly. Blood spurted from the wounds. The panther's reaction could only be an even tighter grip on the bear's throat. 'Let him die now, now,' the panther must have prayed to the Great Spirit. Then the bear, with a mighty effort beyond his own control jerked his legs downward, ripping the panther's underside wide open from top to bottom. And the two then lay still in a great pool of comingled blood.

As all became quiet again, except for the whimper of the kitten in the lair, Milakee went up to survey the scene. The bear was dead. The panther was dead, too, with her teeth still chenched on the throat of her foe.

"Now, Osceola," said the old man, "the panther knew when she made the fight that all the chances were against her survival. But she had to fight to save her kitten. The bear was greedy. He was killing without need. He was taking something that was not his. It was a battle which had to be fought. The Great Spirit called on the panther to fight—to kill, if necessary, to be killed, if that, too, was necessary.

"Osceola, it is better for a man to die faithful to a good cause than to succeed at the cost of deserting what he believes to be right. If in dying faithful to his cause it then becomes strengthened, he does not die. But this experience is only for a few men—only for a few great men."

WAR LEADER

During Osceola's youth, the pressures on his people were becoming increasingly greater. When the United States formally acquired the territory of Florida in July 1821, many circumstances contributed to the rising hostility between the white man and the Indian: (1) Popular General Andrew Jackson, now on the way to the presidency, had achieved much of his fame as an Indian fighter; (2) whites in the neighboring states of Alabama and Georgia could demand help from the United States government now for protection against the Indians, who were said to be "stealing their slaves;" (3) the United States wanted to encourage its white citizens to move into the new territory and develop it. All these resulted in more white-Indian confrontations and more pressure on the Indians to give up land for white settlement.

Spain had conveyed the Florida territory to the United States with the express understanding that "the rights of the Seminoles to their lands be made a part of the . . . transfer, and the Indian population shall be under the protection of the American Government." But with this transfer of Florida from Spain to the United States, thousands of whites—the best and the worst—from bordering states, rushed to the new American territory and the worst of them seized and confiscated, without a vestige of right, the Indians' homes, their well-tilled fields, and their herds of cattle.

To lead any kind of resistance, the Seminoles had many

chiefs whose attitudes widely varied. There was little unity in their loyalties, little strength, or even will to resist.

Treaties that called for removal to the west or into specified Florida areas were worked out and gave some promise of peace from time to time, only to be repudiated by the United States or by the Indians as unauthorized and mere scraps of paper.

The first indication that Osceola was assuming prominence as a leader came following the Payne's Landing council meeting and resulting treaty of 1832. Osceola was present, though this was of no significance to any observer. He was not invited to fix his mark on the treaty because he was not a chief. Colonel James Gadsden, who would later be remembered for the Gadsden Purchase, represented the United States at Payne's Landing in 1832. Gadsden maneuvered a few of the chiefs into signing the treaty document, which stipulated that all of the Indians (many of whom were not represented) living in the Big Swamp area were to be removed to the West "within three years after the ratification of the agreement." Expecting to move as agreed, many of the Indians did not plant crops. The United States government, however, did not move to enforce the agreement, and all the while Osceola was moving to disavow it. From camp to camp, from chief to chief, from council to council, the young Seminole who had become a war chief called for and got more and more united and violent resistance.

When General Wiley Thompson, the United States agent, assembled a large group of Indians to demand that they agree to be moved west no later than the spring of 1835, the Indians held a council of their own. Though not invited to do so, Osceola gave the group a strong challenge to fight—and die if necessary—for what was theirs. He openly repudiated the appeasers among the chiefs, and there were many of them. He established then and there that he was ready to be their leader. Hearing about the meeting and in retaliation, the agent threatened the discontinuance of the aid program. "So be it," said Osceola, acting as spokesman. After this meeting, not only the Indians knew who Osceola was, but so did the whites.

In 1834, another meeting was held and another document was proposed to be signed by the Indian chiefs confirming the Payne's Landing Treaty of 1832. Under this document, various concessions were offered by the United States for the embarkation of the Indians from Tampa by January 15, 1835. Some sixteen sullen and bitter chiefs signed with their marks, thus submitting to the obligation document.

Osceola was present and was invited to come forward and sign. He came forward, but with flashing eyes and uplifted head defiantly shouted: "This is my signature. Rather than act the coward, by signing away the Seminoles' inheritance and taking my people into a strange land, I will fight till the last drop of blood moistens the Seminoles' hunting grounds." With that, he drew his long Spanish knife and drove the blade through the treaty, pinning it to the table, saying, "The land is ours; this is the way I will sign all such treaties." And with this he walked out.

Not all those present were so defiant, however. Charley Emathla, one of the chiefs who had signed the document, prepared to move his tribe to Tampa Bay where they were to board ships for their trip west. In preparation, he and a few of his braves had rounded up and sold the tribe's cattle to General Thompson for a rather substantial sum. On their return from the sale, they were met along the trail by Osceola and his band of braves in war dress, with faces painted the red and black of destruction. Emathla and his braves were felled by a volley of shots. Osceola is said to have then taken the gold which had been collected from General Thompson for the cattle and thrown it on the ground, saying: "It is the price of the Red Man's blood."

Later, Osceola was visiting the trading post of Fort King

for the purpose of buying supplies. While there, he was arrested by order of General Thompson and confined in the nearby fort. He became very violent, storming and screaming abuse and threats against General Thompson. In retaliation, he was chained and beaten and this, to him, was the greatest possible humiliation and hurt. His release later was procured by promises of good behavior, which induced General Thompson to think he had made a convert; but the General was later to learn that this was a grievous error of judgment. Osceola left Fort King with extreme bitterness and a determination to even his score with Thompson.

It was a time of weakening morale among the Seminoles. The weary were gaining ground. More Indian leaders were voluntarily agreeing to pull out in consideration of the money and other help the government offered. But not Osceola. With some bold strokes, he now turned the tide from surrender toward stronger resistance. He commanded raiding parties and engineered ambushes that took heavy tolls of soldiers and white civilians alike. His activity, however, was countered by more troops being moved in. During these battles, Osceola proved himself to be a brave and generous foe. Some reports indicated that he always protected women and children because he did not consider that his battle was with them. He never forgot an act of kindness. He spared foes in battle who previously had done him favors.

Osceola never forgot his special score to settle with General Thompson and he did this with shrewd planning and strong vengeance. With a small group of his most trusted braves, he slipped, undetected, up very close to the United States Agency office next to Fort King. They were armed with rifles and in full war dress and remained carefully concealed. Osceola knew that his enemy Thompson was there and that he was bound to move outside, counting on the safety of the military personnel who manned the fort. Osceola's plan was to wait until most of the soldiers had moved out for a scouting mission, then if Thompson appeared they could shoot and make a quick getaway. The Indians, from their hiding places, watched the soldiers move out on the second day. Then, after dinner, the General and his aide decided to take a stroll outside. The eyes of Osceola followed every movement from the time the General appeared. The other Indians were alerted also, and the rifles were poised and aimed. Upon Osceola's signal, the shots rang out almost as one, and the General fell dead with fourteen lead slugs in his body.

There were many other raids and ambushes. The most severe occurred on the road from Fort Brooke (Tampa) to Fort King (Ocala) in Central Florida on December 28, 1835. Micanopy, head chieftain of the Seminoles, ambushed a force of 110 United States regulars under the command of Major Francis L. Dade and killed all except three. The only one to escape unharmed was Louis Pacheco, a black slave who served as the unit's guide and interpreter. This event, too, was planned by Osceola and doubtless Osceola would have been directly involved but for his almost simultaneous attack on General Thompson. Major Dade and his men had been watched and followed all the way from Fort Brooke by Indian scouts under Osceola's direction.

But the "successes" of the Seminoles were temporary and short-lived. More and more U.S. troops came. The Seminoles were not supplied with either food or arms and soon it became obvious that their survival in Florida was doomed under this kind of pressure. As additional Indian leaders recognized this, they made the best compromises possible and were moved on west or were pressed ever deeper into South Florida.

But Osceola would not give up. He not only took on the United States in his fight, but he also took severe action against his own people who submitted.

In December 1836 General Thomas S. Jesup was the newest general to whom the Government had assigned the task of cleaning out the Seminoles. He was skilled and dedicated to his task. He carefully made his plans to see that the Seminoles were destroyed if they persisted in their determination to stay in Florida. He almost succeeded too.

CAPTURE BY DECEPTION

General Joseph M. Hernandez, General Jesup's chief subordinate, was also an effective soldier and leader. He had captured Chief Philip and his camp. He also surprised and captured Uncle Billy and his followers. All these prisoners had been brought to St. Augustine and confined in Fort Marion (formerly Fort San Marcos). Some of these prisoners suggested that, if properly invited, others of the Seminoles would also give up; and one of their top men, Tomoka John, was released for such a mission. To the surprise of the government people, Tomoka John returned accompanied by Philip's son, Coacoochee, strong friend and supporter of Osceola. Coacoochee had come under a white flag of truce and announced that he expected to leave when he desired. With the promise he would seek to bring other Indians and stolen slaves back with him, he was allowed to leave. He came back, as promised, with other members of Philip's family; but most important of all, he brought word that Osceola, with other chiefs and over a hundred Indians, was just a day's journey away and desired to come in for a conference under a flag of truce.

At about this time, General Jesup had arrived at the fort in St. Augustine, and, upon a discussion of the situation, a plan for receiving Osceola and his group was worked out.

A mile away, Osceola halted his party and sent word ahead that he was prepared for discussions with the United States Army leaders. He gave his exact location and full notice that he would receive them under a flag of truce.

He waited at the place designated, flanked by his most trusted supporters, his bearing erect. But a recent onslaught of malaria fever had left tired lines deep in his still young face. His eyes were large, dark pools reflecting the hate he bore for what his people were being forced to do and the return to slavery the white man was forcing upon his friends, the black people. There was also the yearning that life could be peaceful, but not at the crucial price the white man with the weight of superior forces was demanding. There was confidence that his white flag truce symbol would be honored, but doubts which could not be ignored in light of his weakness and their strength.

Word came that Hernandez was coming and the Indians showed more tenseness. The General moved into the clearing flanked by several aides. He walked up to the standing Indians, noting carefully the flag of truce over Osceola's head, and asked the purpose of the conference. Responding, Osceola first made it clear that they had not come to surrender, but that they had come hoping to make peace. Hernandez inquired about other chiefs he had hoped would be present. It was explained that these were ill and could not attend, that they would come later. Hernandez then rebuked the Indians for past deceptions and stated it would be necessary for all the Indians present to come with him into the fort. To this, the Indians replied, "We will have to see about that."

These were the hostile words that triggered the trap. Hernandez called to his men and they came from the trees and brush on all sides—secretly they had surrounded the entire force of Indians. They now rushed in, as planned, with rifles fixed, and made the capture. Every Indian had his rifle nearby, loaded, just in case of treachery, but not one had the opportunity to use it. Fourteen chiefs, seventy-one warriors, six women, four Negroes, and forty-seven rifles, were taken to Fort Marion. Osceola was the big prize, and it gladdened General Jesup's heart to take him, by fair means or foul. As Osceola rode his horse into St. Augustine side by side with an Army officer, he was still a leader proud of his cause. Someone watching them go by remarked that Osceola's bearing was more like the captor than the captive. But the hopes within him were now dimmed and the fever was rising.

THE VALLEY OF THE SHADOW

The capture of Osceola was followed by an intensive round-up operation by General Jesup and his soldiers. With the word out that the great Osceola had been captured, other Indian leaders came to terms. Some agreed to embarkation, others were offered lands south of a line from Tampa Bay due east to the Atlantic for their own, but this was never carried out.

There was a breakout of Indians held at Fort Marion, and a sizeable number escaped, Coacoochee among them. Osceola had no part in this, and apparently this was his choice. When questioned as to why he did not make his escape, as did other chiefs, he is said to have replied: "I have done nothing to be ashamed of; it is for those to feel shame who entrapped me." He seemed resigned, and this feeling likely was in part due to his illness, which was getting worse.

Early one evening, as the twilight was leaning toward darkness, Osceola heard from far away a familiar call. It was the night bird call "purp-pur-reeb." Moving toward an opening, he gave an answering whistle. He was not surprised to learn an hour or so later that Milakee had come to the fort and voluntarily given himself up, and his heart was warmed.

Soon word came that the whole remaining Seminole group at Fort Marion would be removed by steamship to Fort Moultrie, at Charleston. They embarked on the S.S. *Poinsett* for Charleston on January 1, 1838—five chiefs, including Osceola, 116 warriors, 82 women and children. After arrival there, Osceola was allowed freedom of the enclosure, and he was joined by his two wives and two children.

Dr. Frederick Weedon, who was surgeon of the Fort Marion Post and had attended Osceola there, was of the opinion that his patient could not live more than a few weeks, and he sought to have Osceola kept at Fort Marion hoping his health would improve. His suggestion was rejected because of a continuing fear by the Army that the Indians would make some drastic effort to free him if he continued so near. Also, it was feared that if he died there this might trigger a strong retaliation from the Indians against the whites and a hardening of the resistance toward removal. Weedon then asked to be allowed to accompany Osceola to Charleston, where he could continue to look after him; and this was agreed to by the authorities.

Later the artist George Catlin, learning of Osceola's confinement in Fort Moultrie, obtained the consent of officials and Osceola to come and paint his portrait. While Catlin was working, Osceola had a serious setback. He developed an acute attack of quinsy with a badly inflamed and swelling throat and tonsils. This was an extended complication of his old malaria trouble which had left him in a very weakened condition. Dr. Weedon examined him, expressed deep concern and asked that another doctor be called. When he came, he confirmed Dr. Weedon's diagnosis and both doctors strongly insisted on draining some of Osceola's blood by using leeches applied to his neck and behind his ears.*

When the white doctors insisted on applying the leeches,

* In those days, this was a rather common therapeutic practice resorted to since the early days of the Greeks. It was thought to be a process of draining off the bad element that was inducing the trouble, and thus a means of purification. Hippocrates had described two methods. One was called "wet cupping." A bowl about the size of an egg cup was used. The skin at the point of pain was lightly greased and cut with a lancet or scarified. A piece of fibrous cord was then lighted in the cup and allowed to burn out. Then the cup was clapped tightly to the skin. This created a suction which drew out the blood. The other method was the use of leeches found in the swamps and rivers. They were easily available through apothecary shops of the day and most doctors kept a supply among their equipment. The leech was a black, slimy creature with suction cups at both ends. When applied to the human body, it would stick flat and start withdrawing blood by using both of its ends. When a leech became gorged, it would be removed, drained, then reapplied. Some doctors found that by cutting off one end of the body of a leech after it was applied, it would continue to use the other end and the blood could be collected in a receptacle held under the removed end. The advantage was that there would be no limitation imposed by the amount of blood the leech could hold. But offsetting this was the disadvantage that the leech was doomed to die in this process and could never be reused.

Osceola turned to Milakee and asked his advice. After some whispered comments between the two, the answer was an emphatic "no."

DEATH AND VICTORY

So the death watch began. Sitting on the floor not far from the pad upon which Osceola lay were his two wives and his two children. Milakee was half sitting, half kneeling, so close he reached over and held the dying war chief's hand from time to time. His friend, Dr. Weedon, stood silently watching the pain-wracked body, mercifully hoping that the certain end would come soon for Osceola—patriot, warrior, leader.

Suddenly, all were surprised when Osceola sat up. His head seemed clear, his body under remarkable control. He calmly asked his wives to bring his full dress clothes, the ones he wore in battle. When these came, he stood, put on his shirt with all its bright ornaments, his leggings, and moccasins. He then fixed his belt, which included his bullet pouch and powder horn. The knife that had served his purposes so long and well he placed on the floor. He called for his red paint and a mirror and painted his face one-half red, also his throat and neck and the backs of his hands. He then painted red the handle of his knife, which he placed under his belt. He fixed the turban on his head with his three ostrich plumes. This was his full battle preparation. Feeling weak, he lay back down to recover his strength. Milakee came very close and whispered in his ear: "You have been faithful to our people, Osceola. You are a great leader." The war chief seemed pleased. In moments he stood again. He was confident, relaxed. He held the hands, in turn, of all the chiefs and officers of the post who had now come in at his request, including Doctor Weedon. He whispered something to the members of his family. Then he drew his scalping knife and with head back he struggled to sound his battle cry. Faltering, he motioned for help from those nearby and lay back down on his pad. With his right hand firmly clutching the knife, he put it across his chest. A moment later he smiled and, after a gasp, his breathing stopped. There was no struggle or cry of pain. Osceola—Patriot, Warrior, and strong leader —died January 30, 1838.

Milakee smiled and said, "He is gone. It had to be this way. It will soon be clear to all that he has won his fight in losing. Only a very great leader can do this."

> We call them Savage,
> O, be just
> Their outraged feelings scan
> A voice comes forth—
> 'Tis from the dust—
> The Savage was a man!*

EPILOGUE

Osceola died, but, as prophesied by Milakee, he still lived. His family and the other Seminoles at Fort Moultrie were sent to the Oklahoma reservations, where they became lost to history. But an enormous resentment against his treatment inflamed public opinion in this country and abroad. As a result, the war efforts were not pressed with great vigor in Florida. A long succession of generals came and went. There were no major engagements after Osceola's death, though the struggle went on for years with sporadic raids and retaliation skirmishes. Many of the Seminoles were moved to Oklahoma, others became settled on reservations ultimately consented to and provided by the government. Still others have remained "wild" continuously since.

So Osceola did win in death what he could not win in life—the right of his Indians, who resisted to the end, to stay in Florida and not be sent west; the rights of those who were unwilling to accept life on the reservations to

* Poem inscribed upon monument at Collier Seminole State Park, Marco, Florida.

continue to make their own lives under their own tribal laws and customs and without white hinderance or control. Sadly, however, the price exacted by the white man for this freedom was the acceptance of land of such poor quality that the white man was unwilling to live on it.

Following the death of Osceola, when there were no mourners in the room in which his body lay prepared for burial, Dr. Weedon came in and, unnoticed, cut off Osceola's head. He left it in place with the great young chief's scarf tied around the neck to conceal what he had done. It remained thus until just before the burial of the body near the entrance to Fort Moultrie. Again, when he was alone with the casket, just before removal for the funeral ceremony, Dr. Weedon removed the head and concealed it in his own room. He took it back with him to St. Augustine and after he had embalmed it by a method he worked out himself, he kept it in his home on Bridge Street, where he also had his office.

Why did the doctor commit this act of desecration? In those days, it should be noted in his defense that this was not such an uncommon practice. Heads were considered important for scientific study of the shape and structure of the skull and were taken from very special and unusual people. Five years later, Osceola's head was given by the doctor to a son-in-law, also a doctor, who in turn presented it to Dr. Valentine Mott, a famous surgeon in New York. Dr. Mott kept it for many years with other items of his collection in his pathological museum in New York. In 1866, this museum was badly burned in a fire, and it is assumed that Osceola's head was among the many items destroyed.

What became of Osceola's tutor, the old man Milakee? There is no trace in history of him. But he, too, lives on in Osceola. He gave to him of the Great Spirit's plan, a keen understanding, the courage to fight, and the strength to lead well. It was he who shepherded Osceola into eternity.

AFTERPIECE: OSCEOLA IN CALIFORNIA

During 1945, as a Navy lieutenant, junior grade, I was stationed in Monterey, California for several months in a joint Army-Navy Military Government training program. As an exercise, we scoured the countryside from time to time practicing for our expected ultimate duty. On one of these maneuvers, while we were in a small inland town and taking a brief "at ease," I went into a junky looking antique store just to browse around and kill a little time. Back in a corner, half hidden, my eye caught sight of a familiar face on an old oil painting. It was Osceola and looked like the Catlin portrait I had become familiar with from my earliest Florida history books. I was amazed and quite excited but, of course, pretended to be only casually interested. The proprietor, I soon learned, had no idea who the Indian was or by whom the picture was painted. He had picked it up from some family passing through, for fifty dollars. I could tell it was very old and the notion began to mushroom in my mind that it just might be Catlin's original—which might have become lost—now in my hands. There was no signature but, as I recalled, Catlin, like many other artists of his time, did not sign all of his paintings.

I offered the owner five dollars to hold the painting for two weeks for me and he readily agreed. Then I made careful notes of specific tiny details of the painting, like the number of strands in a stray lock of hair, the shadows on certain ornaments, the arrangement of the three Ostrich feathers in his turban, etc. When I got back to Carmel, where we had rented a house, I hurried down to the town library, anxiously got an encyclopedia, and quickly found Catlin's Osceola. Every detail checked out with my notes and recollection. By this time, I could just visualize the old shop catching fire and burning down before I could get back. Or maybe another interested man would drift in and raise my ante. So, as soon as I could arrange it the next day, I got a leave and headed back with my forty-five dol-

Oil portrait of Osceola by unknown painter or painters in collection of author.

lars. I was greatly relieved and quite excited when I took possession of my now precious painting and headed back with it to Carmel.

The next day, I took it to the art gallery there with a picture print of the Catlin and asked the curator to please tell me what I had. She, too, was perplexed and asked me to leave the painting overnight. She had a board meeting that evening (all members were either artists or connoisseurs of art) and she would have them check it for me.

When I returned the next day, this was the verdict: It

was an original oil painting made about a hundred years before—copied from Catlin's picture. Strangest fact of all, they reported, the picture I had was painted by at least four different artists! They could tell by the stroke styles used that no one painter could have done it. Their assumption was that perhaps there was a teacher with a class of several well-matured painters who took a print of the Catlin picture, then copied it with their individual talents all pooled together.

I have no idea what my picture may be worth now, with a pedigree of that many unknown fathers, nor do I really care, because I happen to like it very much. It hangs in my study at The Grove, and in this way Osceola has been looking over my shoulder while I was writing the foregoing story.

Catlin's Painting of Osceola
Courtesy of National Collection of Fine Arts, Smithsonian Institution

4

☆ ☆ ☆ ☆ ☆

The Wreckers

TO THE FRENCH, they were known as "Filibusters," to the Spanish as "Demons of the Sea," and among themselves as "Brethren of the Coast." To most, however, along the Southern coast of Florida and in the Florida Keys, where they mainly operated, they were known simply as "wreckers." They had their heyday in the decade of the 1850s when, it has been said, during the "busy season" there were between 100 and 150 square-rigged sailing vessels moving in and out of the Florida Straits daily.

The goal of the wreckers was salvage. Many got it legally, but there were times that more got it illegally. Then, too, the lawless operated with degrees of perfidy, some with vulture-like watchfulness for a wrecked carcass subject to be made its prey, others with premeditated effort to induce wrecks and then to kill and steal.

Coconut Grove has the best soil in and around Miami. Its trees and tropical growth of all kinds have a lushness of greens and grow to sizes that tell of countless more years of build-up from inland forest vegetation than is the case of other surrounding lands that have more recently emerged from the sea. People have lived in Coconut Grove longer than elsewhere in the area for this very reason, and their houses are older. The materials from which many of these old houses were made were salvaged from wrecks. Quite a number of them were originally the homes of wreckers too.

I once met an old man in Coconut Grove whose grandfather had been a wrecker, and down the family lines had come tall tales of fact, fringed with fiction, of wreckers and their shenanigans during Florida's early years. Like most old men, he liked to talk, and to have others around listen. And like most old men, too, he seemed to remember more clearly what he had heard seventy-five years ago than what he heard the day before yesterday. When I mentioned this once, he first explained that what he heard in the old days was just more "worth remembering." Then he offered me this technological explanation: he said the human mind is like a computer and it can just hold so much. The facts that go into it when one is young fit easily because there is plenty of room. But as one gets older and the computer fills up, there is not room for much more, though one may try to wedge more and more in. In the cramming process, misses and distortions occur. This is why, he said, one remembers better the things that were stored away earlier than those stored later.

I asked the old man about the wreckers and what he had heard about them over the years. He very quickly put the subject in good order. 'Wrecking' he explained was a very necessary service in the days when the straits and channels were neither marked nor charted and when there was no showing of depths and obstructions. "There were good reasons for having wreckers. They saved a lot of lives and a lot of cargoes," he explained.

I had already done some research down at the Florida State Library and consulted an article on the subject by Dorothy Dodd. It is an exciting part of the history of early Florida, as she explained it.

There were two courses a ship could take in a voyage between Gulf of Mexico ports and the Atlantic coastline of the United States and Europe in the latter part of the eighteenth century and the early part of the nineteenth century. One was through Yucatan Pass between Cuba and Mexico. This course generally was avoided because it added many extra miles to the voyage. Also, adverse winds and currents along this route prevailed eight months of the year. The other, more favored course was through the Florida Straits, a channel between forty-five to eighty miles in width that stretches the length of the Florida Keys between Marquesas Key, which is about twenty-five miles west of Key West, and Virginia Key, which is across Biscayne Bay from Miami. On the western boundary of the straits, a reef of shoals and ledges of sand, rocks, and coral parallel the keys and lie from one to twenty feet beneath the water, waiting like submerged monsters with claws eager to tear and rip gaping holes in the sides of unsuspecting ships. The southern and eastern side of the straits are encased by the rock-bound coasts of Cuba and the Bahamas.

The combination of a curved channel, the reefs, a gulf stream that sometimes reached eight knots, frequent storms, and inadequate lights and charts made the Florida Straits in the nineteenth century one of the most hazardous areas in the world for navigation by sailing vessels. In fact, in 1849, insurance rates for ships traversing these straits were as high as for ships rounding treacherous Cape Horn. The rates were realistic, too, because the Florida Straits were, in fact, the graveyard of thousands of sailing vessels, and many vessels, sunk where the waters were shallow, became additional uncharted hazards for other vessels.

The legitimate wreckers were sailors who patrolled these waters in search of foundering vessels entrapped by the reefs. They would salvage the cargo and, if possible, the vessel, and take as their reward 30 to 50 percent of the value of the property salvaged. There was real money to be made in the business, and many people with many motives were attracted to it.

The first wreckers were the Calusa Indians who were pre-Columbian inhabitants of South Florida. There were no controlling salvage laws at that time; even if there had been, they would have been ignorant of them. They would plunder the wrecked vessels and often slaughter the

stranded seamen. It took extreme measures, but the Calu-
sas' monopoly came to an end after they were captured, en-
slaved, and sent to Cuba in 1763.

The fishermen and turtlers from the Bahama Islands
moved in quickly to reap the profits of this lawless and lucrative business. By the time Florida became a U. S. territory in 1821, fifty to sixty vessels and more than 500 New
Providence seamen were regularly employed in the wrecking business in the area. They generally took their captured
cargoes to Nassau. In fact, the wrecking business at that
time was the chief economic support of Nassau, bringing
in colonial revenue of £15,000 annually. Increasingly, after
Florida became a U. S. territory, Americans got their
hands into the business of wrecking, believing that the
United States should reap the government benefits, and
United States citizens, the spoils. These steps quickly followed: Key West was established as a port of entry and a
collector was appointed in 1822. In 1823, the Legislative
Council of Florida meeting in St. Augustine under much
pressure passed the territorial Wrecking Act. Under this
law, it was provided that: (1) Salvors of wrecked property
must report immediately to a justice of the peace or notary
public upon returning to port; (2) the officer to whom
the wreck and salvage was reported would assemble a jury
of five to investigate the wrecking and award salvage; (3)
the officer would also see that the award was carried out
and notify the superior court of the district in which the
property was landed.

The members of the delegation from St. Augustine to
the first Territorial Council in Pensacola in 1822, incidentally, did not arrive for the session. They were ship-
wrecked in the Florida Straits on the way.

Wrecking boomed for the next several decades. In 1825,
Key West was the central base for wreckers, but business
was so good that other smaller ports developed almost
solely on wrecking support. One such settlement was at
Indian Key.

The responsible wreckers carried on their work to make money, indeed, but they made a great contribution toward making sailing through the Keys a safer journey, and also by pressing demands for various aids to navigation. In 1826, two lighthouses were constructed, one at Cape Florida and one at Key West. It was ironic that the first ship to bring the construction materials from Boston for these lights was wrecked on the way. Other lights were constructed in the following years. A light boat was outfitted and assigned to be stationed off Carysfort Reef, but on her way there she ran aground and had to be hauled off by wreckers.

Not all wreckers were decent citizens. It has been said that one of the worst groups of wreckers settled in what is sometimes known as the northern fringe of the Spanish Main, in the vicinity of Coconut Grove. I had sought out my old friend there, hoping that he would give me a good picture of the rougher side of the business, as he had grown up so close to it.

So he continued: "Freebooters used to row the four or five miles across Biscayne Bay to Biscayne Key, where they built huge bonfires. The fires attracted the vessels of trade which plied southward holding close inland to avoid the main strength of the northward bound current of the Gulf Stream. The vessels would turn to investigate the light, or would asume it to be a guide, and would smash upon the reefs.

"The scavengers, watching all the time, would then dash out and board the ships, take off the wines and other valuables, get roaring drunk, sometimes kill the men if they resisted and kidnap the women. God only knows what all they did to them. Then, after they sobered up, and usually after the ship had broken up on the reef, they would salvage whatever they could haul in.

"Some say that the light that was built at Cape Florida was actually built by the government at these wreckers' request. After the Federal Government unwittingly ob-

liged, thinking it was erecting a very valuable aid to navigation, the wreckers no longer had to build their bonfires,
for Cape Florida Light served well to attract the vessels to
the treacherous reefs for them.

"Each of the federal agencies (it's now the Coast Guard)
which has controlled the lights has denied this. Yet the fact
remains that by reason of its position, it certainly tended to
draw ships upon the reef. And when the light was de-
commissioned in 1876 it was replaced by Fowey Rock Light
(named for a British ship which foundered on the reef
there) which is ten miles or so farther out to sea.

"I'll tell you something else too. Local pilots engaged to
assure safe passage were time after time bribed to wreck
ships deliberately after they took over. Sometimes, too,
there were agreements between wreckers and crooked masters of wrecked ships to divide up the bounty."

It was this kind of conduct that caused legitimate operators and insurance companies to lobby Congress for a local
court with admiralty jurisdiction; and on May 23, 1828,
Congress established a Superior Court for this purpose in
Key West.

The plan actually worked fine. The new Superior Court
judge immediately sought to exert control over the wreckers at the request of responsible elements, mostly from Key
West. The judge declared that no vessel could be employed
as a wrecker without his approval and that no collusive
agreements could be made between an employee of a
wrecking vessel and the master of the wrecked vessel. This
licensing of wreckers had never been done before in the
United States. The sanctions imposed by the judge for
committing any offense were the suspension of license and
denial of a salvage award. The judges of this court actually,
through the exercise of some legislative and some executive powers, along with their judicial ones, transformed
wrecking into a well-regulated business and helped to
reduce such practices as embezzling wrecked goods, the
voluntary grounding of vessels by pilots, and conspiracies
between wreckers and the wrecked.

A typical wrecking operation would begin with a wrecker becoming informed that a wreck had occurred. The first wrecker to the scene was required to show to the master of the wrecked vessel a copy of his wrecking license and the court's rules of wrecking. The master of the vessel could decline or accept the assistance of that wrecking vessel, or of another one if others were present. If he expressed no preference, the first wrecking vessel on the scene received priority and its master, known as the wreck-master, directed the salvage operation. Other wreckers could be excluded from the operation if the first wrecker could handle the salvage operation alone. He shared the salvage job and his prize with others, however, if the circumstances would require it. After the wrecker or wreckers salvaged all the cargo possible, they would return to Key West to reap the rewards.

Between 1844 and 1859, salvaged vessels and cargoes were valued at approximately $25,000,000. The total paid for salvage was approximately $3,000,000. Thus, the regulated wreckers did perform a very beneficial and useful service.

My Coconut Grove old-timer told me this story: An old Methodist preacher in Key West, one Sunday morning, was holding services in the County Courthouse in Jackson Square which also served as a general place of worship for all denominations.

From his position on the rostrum in the courthouse, which served him as a pulpit, he had a clear view of the ocean behind and over the heads of his congregation. On that particular Sunday morning, he saw a ship drifting dangerously toward the reef.

With one eye on his congregation and the other on the ship, he watched her until he was certain that she would be wrecked upon the reef, and then he began making his plans. For the good preacher, as a side-line, was also the owner and master of a wrecking vessel.

The preacher had in mind the rule, which had been upheld by the United States Court, that gave to the master of the first wrecking vessel to reach a ship in distress the right to direct the salvage operations, which always entitled him to additional compensation.

He knew that if he made the announcement from his pulpit that there was a "wreck ashore," or if, through lack of interest, someone turned around and sounded the alarm, his congregation—most of which was composed of wreckers just like himself—would get out of the church ahead of him and undoubtedly beat him to the lucrative job of wrecking master.

So he took his text from I Corinthians, 9th Chapter, 24th verse: "Know ye not that they which run in a race run all, but one receiveth the prize? So run, that ye may obtain."

Understanding well the gravity of the situation, the pastor launched into his text with great zeal. Descending from the pulpit, he exhorted his congregation to equip themselves for the great race for the prize of eternal salvation. He eased down the aisle, hammering away at his text with vivid illustrations and forceful gestures.

And, just as he reached a point near the rear of the church, and before anyone could get out before him, he suddenly brought his listeners back to earth with the cry, "Wreck ashore!"

As he dashed ahead of them down the steps, he shouted: "Now we will all run a race and see who receiveth the prize."

Just about the entire male population of the congregation was at his heels. However, he had a good start on them and soon reached his schooner and, with his crew, which had been among the congregation, he set sail and managed to reach the wreck in time to become the wrecking master.

Wrecking began to decline as a specific occupation as more lighthouses were erected, more accurate charts were made, and steam navigation increased the maneuverability of ships. In December 1921, 100 years after the United States took control of the Territory of Florida from Spain, the wrecking license register of the court was closed.

5

☆ ☆ ☆ ☆ ☆

The Battle of Natural Bridge

As a boy growing up in Tallahassee, my patriotism was continuously nurtured on the often-retold glories of what happened at Natural Bridge, some thirteen miles south of Tallahassee, during the Civil War. There were many different versions, but in those days they all added up to the fact that our gallant Confederates, young boys and old men, fought against the heaviest odds with superior courage and by their heroism saved Tallahassee from capture by the Yankees. This gave to our town the proud distinction of being the only Southern State Capital east of the Mississippi River that did not fall.

At the beginning of 1865, the prospects for an ultimate Southern victory appeared to be doomed even to ardent sympathizers and many of the valiant soldiers in the Southern cause. At that time, the Federal naval and other armed forces deployed on the West Coast of Florida from Key West to Pensacola were very strong. Sensing what he probably misconceived as a serious weakening of Southern morale at that time, General John Newton, U. S. Army, commanding the district of Key West and Tortugas, felt the time propitious to move with an amphibious operation against what he regarded as vulnerable areas in North Florida. Pursuing his plan during the first days of March, he assembled a large number of ships and personnel in Apalachee Bay out from St. Marks. Newton and his staff developed a complicated plan for assaulting several points with limited personnel, at the same time concentrating a main thrust in the vicinity of St. Marks and moving thence northward along the east bank of the St. Marks River on to Tallahassee, some twenty-four miles inland. The landing was made on March 4, with minor skirmishes which did little to impede its progress. When the troops sought to cross the East River, prior to reaching the St. Marks River, they ran into more substantial resistance; but this was overcome and the force moved on up to the vicinity of Newport, where it was first thought that a crossing of the St. Marks from the east to the west bank could be effected.

In the meantime, word had come to Tallahassee on the fourth of the first landings and of the ominous threat which was developing. General Sam Jones, of the Confederate Army, undertook to put together the forces he could muster to confront the enemy. A creditable job was performed under very difficult circumstances. Rallying to the call were some 700 men, made up of several cavalry companies, a light artillery company, several reserve units, and—most significantly—a company of cadets from the West Florida Seminary, located in Tallahassee. This institution was the forerunner of the present Florida State University. It was coeducational, with an enrollment at that time of about forty boys, of ages from twelve to eighteen, and a few less girls. The school occupied a single building at the location now occupied by the Westcott Building of the University. The reserves were mostly overage or partially disabled men living in that area of North Florida, and some came from South Georgia. Part of their equipment was just what they could bring with them from their homes.

General Jones got part of his force down far enough to be involved in the preliminary contact at East River, and when he realized that he could not stop the enemy at that point, he withdrew as quickly as he could to the community of Newport, several miles north on the St. Marks, where he first thought he would make his stand. He got to this

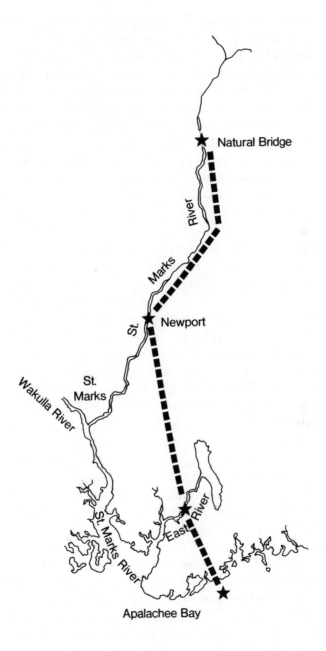

★ Tallahassee

★ Natural Bridge

River

Marks

St.

★ Newport

Wakulla River

St.
Marks

St. Marks River

East River

★

★ Apalachee Bay

Route of Federal march to Natural Bridge.

point time enough in advance of the enemy to destroy a grist mill, a saw mill, and some other lumber shops across the river and to put the bridge there out of immediate use.

The destruction was done as a tactical maneuver to make it easier for his soldiers to get clear shots at the enemy when they approached. Jones realized, however, that the invaders, when resisted at Newport, would be tempted strongly to move on farther north and seek to make a crossing at Natural Bridge, only some three miles distant. Good reasons would seem to dictate such a decision.

Natural Bridge was not a bridge in the literal sense. The river, as it moved toward the sea, simply disappeared there into a sinkhole, then for several hundred yards it moved underground. Then it resurfaced, went on its way a short distance, then repeated the brief disappearing act. The terrain there, although General Newton apparently did not know it, was extremely well-adapted for defensive purposes and poorly suited for an assaulting force. There were sloughs and swampy places over which any movement was almost impossible and between those wet areas was a limited amount of firm, high ground.

General Jones was having his forces continually augmented by new arrivals coming down from Tallahassee, and during the afternoon of the fifth, while some of his troops were making the show of resistance at Newport, his main strength was being diverted and positioned quietly and effectively at Natural Bridge.

As soon as darkness came, General Newton started to move north to make the crossing at Natural Bridge, thus entering the trap being set for him.

The first contact between the opposing forces occurred about four o'clock on the morning of the sixth. The Yankees tried to move across the area using firm ground as they could find it, and they were caught with devastating fire, both from the front and from the expertly-fixed defensive positions on their flanks. The battle continued until about ten or eleven o'clock in the morning, during which time two major attacks were made and repulsed. All the while, more Confederates were arriving in response to the call for help. After a third attack was repulsed, the Federal forces withdrew to some heavy, thick hammock land, from which they launched some lesser attacks; but none of these proved effective.

General Newton, realizing the severe handicap his position placed upon him, and likely overestimating the true Confederate strength, commenced a withdrawal, retracing his route back down the St. Marks River. Some effort was made to harass his retreat with pursuing Confederate attacks, but this operation was thwarted by logs felled across the trail. Efforts to follow were likely also handicapped by the desire of many of the Confederates to get back to Tallahassee to celebrate their extraordinary victory. At any rate, General Newton reached his embarkation point, got his force back aboard the transport ships, and sailed away with little further molestation.

The Capital was saved at the cost of extremely light losses. Only three of the Confederate soldiers were killed and twenty-three wounded. The Federal casualties, on the other hand, were at least ten times as great.

The acclaimed heroes after the fight were the young teenage boys from the Seminary. There were only some twenty-five or thirty of them, but they fought with great courage and effectiveness.

A monument was erected at the site of the battle by the United Daughters of the Confederacy to commemorate the valor displayed there.

*   *   *   *   *

On several occasions in speeches I have referred to this historic event and my association with programs memorializing it. I want to include here several paragraphs quoting some of these remarks. The circumstances I refer to are in large measure truthful, but to some degree they may be apocryphal.

When I was a very young boy, the people from all over our area of Florida would gather at Natural Bridge on Confederate Memorial Day each year for an all-day picnic. Each family would bring a basket of homemade food. Groups generally would pool what they brought. This way everyone had a better variety of choices. Also, those who could only bring light baskets could have a better chance for a real good meal. There was one speech after another and usually a couple of bands that specialized in playing "Dixie," "Swanee River," and other Old South songs. Politicians considered this a good time to announce their candidacy for office. Their style was to "orate" loud and strong, something like our revival preachers used to do.

I remember one old man in particular who was there every year. He usually got introduced from the speaker's platform. His hair was white and he had his beard cut to be like Robert E. Lee's picture in our history book. Now, this old man would always do something that seemed to us children to be very funny. He had a stick he walked around with and he would go up to one place and put the stick down into the ground a little way. Then with one hand on the top of it and while whistling some little tune, he would dance a jig around his stick, singing out, "This is where I stood, this is where I stood." All of us laughed and giggled at him. We thought he was nutty as a fruitcake, but the older folks said he was senile, whatever that meant; we had no idea.

But, you know, I have thought about that old man many times since. He was one of those boys from the Seminary who went down there and fought that battle. He was proud of this and he was proud to put his stick down and say, "This is where I stood."

As I grew older, I quickly came to think he was not senile or crazy at all. In fact, I have found myself hoping that if I manage to live as long as he did, I will be proud like he was to put my stick down and dance and sing and say, "This is where I stood."

I hope that I can go to the Secretary of State's Office, for example, and take down some of the old books where there is recorded the action I took as Governor in any number of matters of importance to the people of Florida, and feel and say with pride, "This is where I stood."

I hope that I can go to the newspaper offices and look back through some of their ancient records that may be yellow with age and find events reported that occurred in my active time and in which I was involved and say, with pride, "This is where I stood."

I hope I can go up to Washington and find the reports and recordings of the work done by that little agency with the big job, the United States Community Relations Service, and also be proud to point to its report of progress in human relations, and say, "This is where I stood."

Judah P. Benjamin
Davis, *Rise and Fall of the Confederate Government*

6

☆ ☆ ☆ ☆ ☆

Judah Philip Benjamin

FROM CONFEDERATE TO QUEEN'S COUNSEL

ONE EVENING PRESIDENT John F. Kennedy entertained all living American winners of Nobel Prizes at a very beautiful dinner in the White House. It was a most significant occasion, bringing all these extraordinary people together at one time and place. In his short talk extending greetings after dinner, the President remarked that this was the most brains ever assembled in the White House at one time since Thomas Jefferson dined there alone.

Not meaning to detract from Jefferson, in a personal conversation a short time later I asked the President if he had ever read the story of Judah P. Benjamin. He had and remembered its broad outlines. I wish to tell the story of this brilliant man not only because he remains largely unknown still, but because he came our way in Florida under most unusual and difficult circumstances.

Judah Benjamin was of Spanish-Jewish ancestry. He came from the same racial stock that produced Benjamin Disraeli. He was born at Saint Croix in the Virgin Islands on August 6, 1811. This was in the period described by a Danish writer as the "troubled years" of those sparkling gem-like islands set in the warm, translucent southern sea. The elder Benjamins found it difficult to raise their family there, and in 1813 they sailed to Wilmington, North Carolina, to join an uncle of Mrs. Benjamin's, Jacob

73

Levy, in what seemed to be a more hopeful venture. From there, the family moved to Fayetteville in 1817, where Uncle Jacob had substantial real estate holdings. But success did not come here either, and soon another move was made, this time to Charleston, around 1822.

Charleston made a strong impression on young Judah. As a boy soon to enter his teens, for the first time he came face to face with slavery and strong social class consciousness. The Benjamins did not adhere strongly to orthodox tenets, but, recognizing young Judah's unusual potential, they saw to it that he had the advantage of the best attainable preparatory education, in a local private academy.

In 1825, Judah had completed his preparatory work and was sent to Yale at the age of fourteen. He was required to pass an examination before being allowed to matriculate, but this proved no problem. He was the youngest student in his class and one of the smallest in physical stature. He mastered his freshman work, demonstrating a remarkable intellectual capacity, and made it through his sophomore year, as well as a part of his junior year, with ease. But then, for reasons not clear, but which suggest an unwillingness on his part to endure some stings of prejudice, and even an accusation of dishonesty, he headed for New Orleans alone, where he expected to make his fortune.

He arrived there with five dollars in his pocket and took a job in a mercantile house. One job led to another better one, and all the while he was studying law on the side. At age twenty, he was admitted to the Louisiana Bar, and two months later he married Marie Augustin Natalie St. Martin, a Creole beauty. He had now become twenty-one; she was sixteen. His relations with his wife became quite turbulent and unhappy, but this phase of his life I will not explore further.

His success as a lawyer was extraordinary. Within only a few months, he was appealing cases and arguing with great competence; and these were cases of importance and complexity. In his spare time, he set himself to the tedious task of preparing a digest of Louisiana Supreme Court decisions, which was promptly published. The work proved so popular that a subsequent edition of greatly expanded scope was developed. This, with his success in trial work, greatly enhanced his reputation, and while still in his twenties he came to be judged by his peers as one of the most talented members of the Louisiana Bar.

Benjamin's first entry into politics came with his election as a Whig member of the Louisiana State Legislature. Then, as the decade of the 1840s moved forward, he enjoyed success not only as a lawyer, but went into farming on a large scale, having acquired large sugar plantation holdings. Before the decade was over, he also had been elected to the United States Senate.

He could not have come to the Senate in a more difficult period than those years which led to the War between the States. His abilities were quickly recognized by his colleagues. He could be depended upon to master and do well everything he undertook. He was a splendid speaker, organizing his thoughts well in advance and making his arguments clear, concise, and convincing. During the late winter of 1852–53, President Fillmore nominated him to serve as a justice of the Supreme Court of the United States, the first Jew ever to be so honored. He declined the appointment, however, expressing his own preference for a more active political career.

Jefferson Davis then was serving as U. S. senator from Mississippi, and a warm relationship between the two lawmakers was begun in Washington which became much closer with the events soon to unfold. Another of Benjamin's best friends was Senator David Yulee of Florida. The two found much in common. They were both born in the same year in the Virgin Islands. Both were Jews, both had entered law and politics, both had married Gentile wives.

When war broke out between the states, and Louisiana

seceded, this brought, of course, Benjamin's resignation from the United States Senate. His leaving, like that of other Southern senators, was a sad farewell.

He returned to New Orleans and his law practice, but not for long. Jefferson Davis, the newly-chosen President of the Confederacy, called on him to serve as attorney general in his cabinet, and this called for his removal to Richmond. This proved to be a task of incalculable difficulties, but Benjamin performed his work so well that Davis drafted him to serve in the even more critical position of secretary of war in September of 1861. For a time, he even performed the duties of both positions.

As the problems of maintaining the Confederacy became more and more severe, Benjamin could see and understand them, and it was largely through his genius that the weak government was kept in the strongest possible posture. It became clear that Davis depended on him more than upon any other man, actually demanding and receiving from him efforts greater than the combined input of many of his other high ranking and most trusted helpers.

When it appeared that the Southern cause would be doomed without more effective help from foreign sources, Benjamin was named secretary of state so that the best possible talent could be utilized in this sensitive position. In this role, also, Benjamin displayed his characteristic skill. In 1865, of course, failure of the Confederacy was a practical certainty.

THE FLIGHT

Richmond, in the early spring of 1865, gave every indication of impending disaster. The weather seemed always to be cloudy and raining, usually in sharp, stinging gusts, leaving large pools of wet mud soggy in the streets. Grant's Army had broken through Lee's thinly-held lines and Sherman was moving with little hindrance into North Carolina. Benjamin, with all his other duties, worked feverishly with plans for the government leaders to escape to the south and avoid capture.

General Lee, on April 1, sent word to President Davis that he was preparing to evacuate his position on the James River at once. This made it certain that Richmond would have to be abandoned. On Sunday, soon after 11:00 P.M., a train bearing Davis, Benjamin, and other officials pulled out for Danville. It could go no faster than ten miles per hour but arrived at Danville at 3:00 P.M. the next day.

The officials were quartered there, and news soon came of Lee's surrender. The presidential party was then privately transported to Greensboro, North Carolina, some fifty miles to the south, where a fateful cabinet meeting was held. Two generals reported that the Confederacy had only 25,000 men remaining in the field.

In all the agony of this tortuous trip, Benjamin felt a duty to try to keep up the spirits of the weary, frustrated group. When the silence of doom would hang heavy, it was Benjamin whose cheerful voice and manner would start a laugh. He would recite from memory long passages of poetry. His favorite seemed to be Tennyson's "Ode on the Death of the Duke of Wellington."

The men took off southward in their horse-drawn carriages with a faithful cavalry escort; and after slogging through mud at a slow rate, they finally arrived at Charlotte, North Carolina. While the group was here, word came of the assassination of President Lincoln. And it was there that Jefferson Davis announced a plan for reestablishing the Confederacy west of the Mississippi. The trip southward resumed. At Abbeville, South Carolina, the last council of war was held. Davis pleaded for continuing the struggle, but he was greeted only with silence, and later he was convinced by the others of the futility of his hopes.

The group was deeply depressed and fears of their imminent capture increased as reports came to them of groups of Yankee soldiers who were scouring the country searching for them. When Davis insisted upon heading west, Benjamin went to him and told him that he could see no way of serving the cause further and asked for his consent to break off and try to make a separate escape through Florida. This request was granted, and Benjamin, alone, carrying only what he wore in the way of clothing, parted from the President near Washington, Georgia, and headed south on his horse.

He decided first to disguise himself as a traveling Frenchman; and, securing a new horse and buggy, he took to the road under the assumed name of "Monsieur Banfal." He pretended not to speak English and engaged an interpreter. A week later, Benjamin learned of Davis's capture, and the next day he crossed the border of Georgia into less populous Florida. Here, he changed his disguise to that of a South Carolina farmer looking for new land on which he and some friends could settle. He had a farmer's wife make him a suit of rough farmworking clothes; and in this effective disguise, avoiding the larger towns, he made his way down to Central Florida. Fearing the Atlantic Coast southward because of well-known marine patrol activity in and around all that area, he decided his chances would be better to work his way to the West Florida Coast.

The next record of Benjamin's travel experiences shows him to be proceeding on a back road riding a mule in what is now Polk County. He is reported to have come to a place where several different trails led in different directions, and he had no way of knowing where any one of them would lead. Unwilling to make an immediate decision, he went into the bushes and lay down for a quick nap. He was awakened by a call, "Hi for Jeff!" But he could see no one close by. The sound was repeated several times before he discerned that it came from a parrot perched high in a tree nearby. Benjamin concluded that the parrot must have strayed from a home of strong southern sympathies and that the bird might lead him to help

if he could make him go home. He took rocks and when
he hit the bird it took off in fright. Benjamin followed,
and, as he had calculated, the house he came to sheltered
friends who were happy to help him.

Major John T. Lesley of Tampa helped Benjamin to
reach the Manatee River. Lesley knew the country and
manner of the people of the area well. He took Benjamin
to the beautiful home built by Major Robert Gamble
near the river and introduced him as Mr. Howard. Here,
Benjamin found sanctuary and safety for several weeks,
with Captain Archibald McNeil and his family. Captain
McNeil, who had been a Confederate commissary agent,
also was fearful of being captured by the Yankees. Both
men had a narrow escape when a group of Union soldiers
raided the house one afternoon. There had been no warning, but the two fugitives were able to slip out the back
door into a grove, barely avoiding detection and capture.
This close call made Benjamin all the more anxious to
move on. With a boat he got from Captain John Curry,
he crossed the river to the home of Captain Fred Tresca,
who was familiar with the inland water routes down the
West Coast. For nearly two weeks, arrangements were
being made by which he could continue his flight.

Captain Curry had obtained a yawl which had been
sunk in a creek for two years to conceal it from the enemy.
In this boat, Benjamin, with Captain Tresca and one H. A.
McLeod, set out down Sarasota Bay. Great skill was required to navigate the boat in this area, but this was supplied largely by McLeod, an able boat handler and seaman.
For two weeks they continued slowly, stopping to go ashore
for water and provisions. They lived, in large part, off of
the land of the seashore, turtle eggs and crabs. Coconuts
proved of great value in their diet. Again, they had a narrow escape from capture. They sighted a Federal gunboat
just as it was lowering a small boat to chase them. Running
their own boat into Gasparilla Pass, they concealed themselves in thick mangrove shore growth. The pursuing boat

came so close that the voices of the Yankees could be clearly heard. Benjamin and his fellow fugitives were so fearful that their pursuers were continuing to lurk nearby that they stayed concealed for two days before venturing out.

Still farther down the coast, they encountered another Federal gunboat. This time there was no time or place to hide. Captain Tresca ordered Benjamin to put on a cook's apron and cap and to busy himself with some cooking chores, and Benjamin played the role superbly, with grease spots and gusto. Their boat was boarded and Tresca questioned. He responded that they were doing some fishing to supply some men who were stationed nearby and, seeing tackle and other fishing gear aboard, the Federals accepted the story as plausible. One of the Yankees remarked, as an aside, after observing Benjamin at his cooking duties, that in all his lifetime this was the first time he had ever seen a Jew doing common work like that.

About July 7, the little boat had reached Knight Key at the Southern end of Florida. Here, they traded the yawl for a larger boat, the *Blonde*, and struck out for Bimini in the Atlantic 125 miles east. It was not smooth sailing. They encountered severe storms, water-spouts, and almost drowned. Benjamin himself described this phase of the journey in a letter with these words:

> I did not write you in my last of the narrow escape I had from water-spouts when in my little boat at sea. I had never seen a water-spout, and often expressed a desire to be witness of so striking a phenomenon. I got, however, more than I bargained for. On the night before I reached Bemini, after a day of intense heat, the entire horizon was black with squalls. We took in our sail, unstepped the mast, and as we were on soundings, we let go the anchor in order to ride out the squalls in safety. They were forming all around us, and as there was no wind, it was impossible to tell which of them would strike us. At about nine o'clock, however, a very heavy, lurid cloud in the west dipped down toward the sea and in a single minute two large water-spouts were formed, and the wind began blowing furiously directly toward us, bringing the water-spouts in a straight line for our boat. They were at the

distance of a couple of miles, and did not seem to travel very fast. The furious whirl of the water could be distinctly heard, as in a long waving column that swayed about in the breeze and extended from the ocean up into the cloud, the spouts advanced in their course. If they had struck us we would have been swamped in a second, but before they reached us the main squall was upon us with such a tremendous blast of wind and rain combined that it was impossible to face the drops of water which were driven into our eyes with such violence as to compel us instantly to turn our backs to it, while it seemed that the force of the wind was so great that it would press our little boat bodily down into the sea. The waves were not high, the strength of the blast being such as to keep the surface of the water compressed. On turning our backs to this tremendous squall, judge of our dismay on seeing another water-spout formed in another squall in the east, also travelling directly toward us, although the wind was blowing with such fury from the west. There must have been contrary currents at different heights in the air, and we had scarcely caught sight of this new danger, when the two spouts first seen passed our boat at a distance of about one hundred yards (separated from each other by about a quarter of a mile), tearing up the whole surface of the sea as they passed, and whirling it furiously into the clouds, with a roar such as is heard at the foot of the Niagara Falls. The western blast soon reached the spout that had been coming toward us from the east and checked its career. It wavered and broke, and the two other spouts continued their awful race across the ocean until we lost sight of them in the blackness of the horizon. A quarter of an hour after, all was calm and still, and our boat was lazily heaving and setting on the long swell of the Bahama Sea. It was a scene and picture that has long become photographed into my brain, and that I can never forget.

Benjamin reached Bimini on July 10. Now, he thought he was safe at last, and took passage soon for Nassau on a small sloop. The morning after departure, however, the sloop foundered thirty-five miles offshore and sank in a matter of moments. Benjamin barely managed to get into a small skiff which the sloop had in tow before the larger vessel went to the bottom. The skiff was leaky, had one oar, no provisions, and only five inches of it was above the water level. Its occupants were Benjamin and three Negroes. Fortunately, the sea was calm. They well knew that with the slightest roughness of the sea they would go down with no chance of survival. That is, unless a choice was made about how the load could best be lightened, and Benjamin likely realized that his minority status would not be to his advantage in settling this question.

But the weather stayed very calm and they slowly proceeded toward land. About eleven o'clock, they sighted a vessel in the distance which they felt they could reach if the weather remained calm. By five in the afternoon, they made it and were taken aboard the British Lighthouse Yacht *Georgina* and taken back to Bimini. Here, Benjamin was reunited with Tresca and McLeod, who later took him safely to Nassau. From Nassau, he proceeded to Havana and from there to England.

The facts are not clear as to how much gold Benjamin carried with him on his flight or where it came from. There were many rumors that the whole Confederate cabinet absconded with gold of various estimates in value. It is certainly true that Benjamin had gold from some source and he likely could never have escaped without it. Along the way he paid those who helped him liberally with gold. Mr. McLeod is reported to have received $1,500. He left $900 to be sent to his sisters in Georgia. But apparently, most of his money was paid out for services of all kinds by the time he reached Havana.

As he journeyed to England, however, he assumed correctly that he would find a resource there that would sustain him. Before the Confederacy collapsed he had shipped 500 bales of his own cotton there for sale and he had been assured the proceeds were being held for him.

A NEW CAREER

Benjamin was warmly received in London. He had developed contacts there among important people. The

Confederate cause had been popular and while his role in the struggle was not understood by the masses, it was understood by many and his reputation for high competence had preceded him.

Vigorously, he set himself to the difficult task of developing a position in the legal profession. He was confronted with enormous handicaps: his "foreign" background, his extremely limited resources of money and credit, and his age. He was now fifty-five, not a propitious age for an average person to start a new career in a new country. But there was nothing average about Judah P. Benjamin.

Before he arrived, he had acquired, through his broad scope of reading and study, a very good understanding of the basics of the English legal system and knowledge of the ways it differed from practice in the United States. The *London Times* had commented at the time that Benjamin had "now sat down quietly to qualify himself to earn his bread." But the *Times* was not aware of how near he had arrived toward this point before he had started.

Benjamin could not be admitted to practice as a barrister until he had served an apprenticeship. He was fortunate to be accepted into a leading firm for this preparation. Before his first year was out, he had established himself as a lawyer of great merit and had become a barrister. Age was far less an obstacle to success in England than in America. Many of England's leaders were very old, while American leaders were mostly young.

At first, he offended the judges by brash over-confidence in his knowledge of the law. This was not good manners in England, where extreme courtesy and deference were expected from those addressing the bench; and Benjamin learned to accommodate himself more to this tradition.

His skill lay in the directness of his argument, in stating his case clearly, briefly, eloquently. His varied experience and comprehensive knowledge of foreign laws and customs proved of great help. No one at the bar excelled him in the easy command of English, French, Latin and Spanish. He had an engaging way of addressing the court as if it were impossible for him to lose. Dr. Robert D. Meade, in his book *Judah P. Benjamin, Confederate Statesman,* writes:

> One of the first firms Benjamin represented in England was an old established marine-insurance company. When just before its annual meeting the company decided to have its usually lengthy rules revised, its two regular counsel refused to do the work in so short a time despite the sizable fee. The assignment was then given to Benjamin and the instructions were sent him late one evening. Most lawyers would have had to study the rules of similar organizations in order to collate them and exhaust all the sources of improvement. But not Benjamin!

> He got up for an early breakfast, sat down to his task, and worked steadily, not stopping for lunch. By eight o'clock that evening—his dinner hour—he had completed the new set of rules. And then wrote them out "in his own neat hand *currente calamo,* with scarce an alteration or correction from beginning to end, as if he had been composing a poem."

> "I doubt if any draughtsman within the walls of the two Temples could have done this so efficiently within the same time," Charles Pollock declared.

Others sang his praises in similar terms. From across the sea in the United States word was beginning to spread that Benjamin had become a very distinguished barrister in the mother country.

In these early years in England, Benjamin also became interested in additional writing. In 1868, he published a new work first given the lengthy title *A Treatise on the Law of Sale of Personal Property, with Reference to the American Decisions to the French Code and Civil Law.* (The title was later reduced to *Benjamin on Sales.*) It became an instant success and is included to this day in almost every large law library in the English-speaking world.

By early 1870, Benjamin was made a Queen's Counsel for Lancaster. He received other awards never before accorded to an American and many which were given to few barristers at the English Bar.

In 1872, he was given a "patent of precedence," the first ever presented to a former American lawyer. It was awarded him after his notable appearance in the House of Lords in *Potter v. Rankin,* even though he lost the case. This "patent of precedence" given by the Queen gave him rank above all future queen's counsel and all sergants at law.

Benjamin, because of ill health which had troubled him often during his later years, and a desire to spend his remaining years with his wife in Paris, announced his permanent retirement in 1883. To celebrate the occasion, a warm farewell banquet was given in his honor in London. No American had ever been honored by an occasion so dazzling. It was attended by the greatest and most influential barristers of all England, the lord chancellor, judges from all the courts of the judiciary, and members of the Queen's Council. There was a great outpouring of tributes of deep respect and love by those who had come to know and appreciate his talents, character, and friendship.

Benjamin never returned to the United States. He died on May 6, 1884, in Paris, where he is buried.

This man, whom an admiring Abraham Lincoln had called the "smartest" of all the officials in the Richmond revolutionary government, had proved by an active lifetime that he would ask no quarter in any contest.

*   *   *   *   *

To honor Benjamin's memory and service, the State of Florida has acquired the Gamble Mansion near Bradenton where he found sanctuary on our soil, and maintains it as a museum and park for the enjoyment of its citizens and other visitors.

INTERLUDE:

Reflections of a Part-Time Beachcomber

GROWING UP

I was a white boy
Around twelve or thirteen
Growing up with stout heart
And eager-face,
In a southern town
That was creaking along
At a horse and buggy pace.
Streamers of tired Spanish moss
Hung down everywhere
From old oak limbs,
Framing here and there
A few grand houses
That gave distinction to the place.
The thinking of the people
Was about the same,
Take it or leave it—
Some hope, but more despair,
Not much seemed to happen
To shake the humdrum fare.

In our town the white masses,
Belonged to three classes,
According to some old wit or fool:
There were the "golddusters",
Rich as Croesus;
The "hominy huskers",

Long on Jesus;
The "depot greasers",
Unwashed, unshaved and unschooled.
From my window of life
The golddusters went to and from
Their fine banks
And glittering parties,
Little noticed by
The hominy huskers,
Who stuck close
To their stores,
Untidy offices,
And work benches.
The filthy greasers
Messed up the courthouse
Spitting their tobacco juice
On the walls and floors
And telling tall tales
Of smart lawyers,
And smarter whores.

Many black people
Lived out their deep-rutted
Lives there too.
We liked them.
They did most of the heavy
And dirty work
At a slow pace
And for low pay,
Our best jokes
Came from their funny ways
Of shanty living,
And graveyard ghosts.
The black children
Went to separate schools,
Meager in teaching,
But strong in rules

About it being best
For both races,
If they would always
Stay in their places.

Sundays most blacks went
To little wooden churches
White painted
With two narrow windows
On each side.
There they would stomp and screech
As they gave praise
To the mighty God
Within their small reach.
For the hominy huskers
Around my age
One of our favorite adventures
Was to hide in the bushes
Outside one of these churches
On a moonlit night—
And, peering through
A window's narrow slot
Watch a performance
I never forgot.
It all started slowly,
With some talk,
But mostly singing,
And the rhythmic patting of feet.
Increasingly, the gravel voiced preacher
Would chant his calls
For more work at the judgment seat.
And approving responses
Would come back—
Strong "Amens", Hallelujahs",
And "Yes brothers"
All true to the beat.
It would all work up

To a grand finale
Of incredible din,
With cymbals crashing
And shouts of praise,
As sister after sister
Came to the last phase.
Falling to the floor
In an orgy of screams,
And weird body contortions,
And twitching and gasping
Near exhaustion,
She would "come through".
This brought a glorious release
From the clutches of hell,
And a "welcome in"
To the wonders of God's kingdom,
Washed clean of all sin.

One Saturday in late July,
School was out
And I was working,
Clerking in a grocery store.
A man came in—
A black man from the country,
We all knew as "Uncle Ben".
His overalls were frayed from age,
And countless back yard scrubbings.
They hung precariously
From only one
Still game suspender.
Dry old leather in the face,
His shoulders were stooped
From years of cotton picking,
And mule wagon sitting
In the steaming summer sun.

Uncle Ben specially wanted me
To wait on him.

He seemed to like me,
And I was proud
Of this distinction.
All he wanted
Was whispered low:
A dime's worth of lard
In a paper tray
And over this a nickel's worth
Of black cane syrup
From the barrel.
When I gave him
This strange concoction
He sat on a crate,
And with a stick for a spoon
Started his meal.
A moment or two later
I made a final check,
Before taking up another chore,
And suddenly,
I started shrieking
"Uncle Ben,
Your tray is leaking!"
(That nasty stuff was oozing
Down his trouser leg
And the sight of it
Upset me more
Than it did him.)
I got a cloth,
And taking the faulty tray,
Started cleaning away.
He didn't move or speak at all,
But in his eyes—
Tired and weak—
There was a tear
About to fall.
Then I gave him a new serving
In a new tray,

Of the same sweet grease,
All compliments of the store.
He seemed pleased,
Wanting nothing more.

                    *   *   *   *   *

Many years have stretched out
Since this event.
Years of experience
And searching
For a conscience,
In private living
And government.
I still see Uncle Ben
On that box now as then.
The memory won't go away.
But in the light of events
That have transpired since,
I ask myself now:
Why was my brother so poor?
Why was this the best meal
He could get?
Eating like this
I wonder now
How many more years
Could his life have run?
How many children did he
Leave at home that day
Running naked in the sun—
Deep in the darkness of ignorance,
And sickness,
Walled in from hope?

Back then
We didn't have any lynchings
In our town.
Oh, a band of greasers
Every now and then,

After some raping,
Or knifing or
Shot gun shooting,
Would take things
Into their own hands—
A few beatings—
But that was all.

No lynchings?
I take that back.
The black people—
All the Bens
And their brothers and sisters
That we called
Uncle and Auntie,
Never Mrs. or Mister,
People who came to
Our back doors,
And stayed behind signs
Marked "Colored";
And bent their children
To the same cruel yoke
Of deprivation
And humiliation—

Well, I now feel
That we lynched them
All right,
In all these ways,
Every day,
Every night.
          *   *   *   *   *

God, help me to see
Beyond the tear
That needs drying,
Also the cause of the crying.
Keep me from feeling again,
As that day,

That I have done well enough,
By just stopping
A hole in a tray.

SAND DUNES

I love the sand dunes,
The kind with green splotched
Transparent veils
That cover the sand,
Round and smooth underneath
Like a woman's breast.

I like to share the lee side
With the waving sea oats.
Then anxiously I look
On the sea side
For the green turtle's nest.

Sand dunes stand for more
Than the joy they give
To the nature lover's eye.
They are the foundation
For the whole seashore.
Here a thousand living things
Crawl and run before
The sea gull's searching cry.

Sand dunes hold back
The wind and the sea
From spoiling the inland vegetation,
And all that this means
For you and me.

So when I see a bulldozer
Leveling off a sand dune
For some new housing start,
Or see some beach rider
Tearing one apart,
I think the hurt must go deep
Right into God's own heart.

BEACH WALK

Walking on a beach early in the morning a man gets to notice many strange things. Of course, there is the fire red sun when it first peeps up far out on the horizon of the sea, and the magnificence this brings to the clouds of all sizes and shapes above. No two mornings are the same so one can always look forward to a new spectacular. That is, if the clouds are not so heavy that they blot out the sun altogether.

Then there are the shell creatures, some scurrying around, others just lying very still, perhaps playing possum.

And the birds, the little fellows on toothpick legs with such remarkable knee action. The line of their back stays evenly horizontal with the sand and yet those legs go so fast they become a blur. The bigger flyers come in also. Some we call skimmers. They have long wing spreads and, looking for their food, they fly only a foot or so over the line where the wave reaches farthest up on the shore. Other large birds including the pelican use a different approach. They fly thirty feet or so above the water and dive bomb for their food. You would think that they would injure themselves upon such a crash into the sea, but they don't. In fact, more often than not they come up with a wiggling fish in their beak.

From the beach a man also can see strange things on the high land back from the sea. For example, on my walks I always notice an isolated pine tree. There is no other tree within hundreds of yards. It seems brave standing there with its small cluster of limbs more like a hat than a dress. And I think: if this tree can grow there, taking all the pressure the wind can offer, year in and year out, why aren't there others in that area? It couldn't be because of a lack of seed because this tree itself drops hundreds, maybe thousands every season.

I asked a tree expert about this once and he said that some species of pine depend upon a long tap root which goes straight down about as far as the tree goes up. And I think that far underneath my lonesome tree there must be a pool of fresh water that nourishes it. Any new seedlings that may start must die before their roots can get down that far.

This reminds me of some people I know. They have something very special that enables them to stand high though all around there is a desert of people sick with power madness, and lust for material things and shallow satisfactions. And, you know, there is no doubt in my mind that people who are loners in their beliefs and still grow high against the wind, also have something very special deep down. Like the expert said about the tree, I believe there is a deep pool of something from which they draw the substance that sustains them. Isn't this what we can call faith?

Getting back to the tree. If the seedlings' roots cannot grow down to reach the pool, how did the one lone tree make it? The only answer must be that this special tree gave something extra in its effort that the others would not. This tree would not take defeat. It didn't mind being alone, it desperately wanted to live and to stand high.

And that goes for people too. One has to want faith very badly to reach it.

That's why I feel a little humble as I walk by that tree that stands there lonesome, yet proud.

THE SHELL

Once I was strolling on the beach at Dog Island. It was a cool, late afternoon and the tide was low, providing a perfect time and place for wading in and out of countless ankle deep pools, the legacy of the last tide that receded from the shore. This is when shell-finding is best and our little house there, like the houses of our neighbors, is well supplied in almost every nook and cranny from countless barefoot expeditions of this kind.

On this afternoon I also had the pleasure of the company of my six year old granddaughter, Jane Brevard Aurell. The world just held the two of us as in our grubby clothes and with our knock-around sticks, we meandered in and out investigating little things, picking up, putting in our bag, or putting back down. What we did, what we said, on occasions like this was just what came naturally, no rules, no inhibitions, no affectations.

As usual, I carried the bag for our treasures and as she found something she wanted to take home and keep she would show it to me eagerly, and I would put it away.

On this afternoon she came up once quite excited over a find. With eyes sparkling she held it forth and said, "Granddaddy, here is a beautiful shell."

I replied with some deference, but firmly, "Honey, it is pretty but we don't want to keep that one, it has a hole in it."

She was crestfallen. "But look, Granddaddy, how pretty it is here, and here, and here,'" she kept pointing to other places on the shell where it was indeed pretty. "Don't look at the hole," she insisted.

"Okay," I yielded, "we will take it in." Then she was off and away hunting for another.

On another walk, months later, when I was alone on the beach, I thought again of this experience and it occurred to me that I was looking at Jane Brevard's shell from the wrong end of the telescope. I was seeing only the hole. When I looked from the right end, something much larger loomed into view.

There are many *people* with holes in their shells—physical defects, mental defects, personality defects. Sadly, it is the nature of so many of us to see only the hole and reject them when usually there is much beyond this that is beautiful.

I once asked a blind man what was the greatest obstacle he felt he had to overcome. I thought he would say walking across a busy street, or preparing his food, or something physical like this. But he said, "My greatest handicap is that everybody I talk to just thinks of me as a blind man. They are sympathetic, but it is not sympathy I need most, it is the understanding by people that I am not just a blind man. I am a man *with just one thing wrong.* There are so many other ways in which I am not handicapped. If they could just see these over and beyond my blindness."

Consider the matter in an even larger focus. We all know people who have beliefs with which we do not agree. Are we not often prone to see a difference like this as a hole, and allow our whole attitude toward the person to be shaped by our hostile reaction to this one thing? Also, isn't this intolerance the raw makings of bigotry—and prejudice?

Wasn't it the Nazarene who said that the best way to make the kingdom of heaven is to be like a child? Something like that.

Jane Brevard, I am glad you saw the beautiful parts of that shell and told me not to look so hard at the hole.

PAPA AND JOE NATHAN

My father lived to be eighty-four. He worked hard running first one and then another grocery store in Tallahassee from the time he was grown until he was in his forties. Then a doctor told him his heart was faulty and to slow down. With a large family (Mama and six children), he couldn't retire completely, so he changed his work to something less arduous—buying and selling real estate, building little houses on lots he acquired, and selling them. He liked this and, with less labor, earned more income. So, even if he did not have a heart attack (and it seemed doubtful to him in his later years that the doctor had been correct), the diagnosis likely proved rather fortunate for him and his family.

I have never known a man who loved to fish more or one who could fish better. Some of my earliest recollections of him are "out on a fish pond," as Mama used to say. By the time I was eight, he would often take me along, and I would have the special privilege of paddling the boat for him. Usually, we were accompanied by first one fishing crony and then another. We would usually go at night; Lake Jackson was his favorite place. This lake has a large main body with a number of "arms." It was just a short ride in our Ford, for the arms reached in very close to town. Meginnis Arm and Ford's Arm were two of our favorite places.

After dark, but before the moon came up, we would go out from a "landing" in a homemade wooden boat which was kept there. There was usually a pole in the boat which Papa would use to push out through the grass until we reached the bonnet-fringed outer edge and deeper water. This was where Papa liked to start fishing, and I would then take over and do the paddling from the back seat.

The sounds of the night on the lake will always fill a special chamber of my memory. The bullfrogs made the most noise doing their individual raucous things, some playing on bass horns, others croaking in higher keys.

There was no coordination, but they were accompanied by the continuing chatter and din of the crickets. Papa said the crickets did all this by scratching their back feet together, but to this day I can't see how this was possible. Occasionally, we would unroost a bird from a low bush and he would screech his disgust over our poaching in his yard. Up on the rising hills above the lake in the woods, there was usually a hoot owl carrying on a dialogue with a friend across the lake in another patch of woods beyond the stretching corn fields.

My paddle would add its dip, trickle, and bubble as I carefully placed it into the black water, carefully pulling it up close against the side of the boat with my right hand, holding it firmly there, and then with a smooth pushing of my left arm and pulling of my right, move the boat quietly forward. Papa had taught me how to do this without banging the paddle on the boat and how to stay on course without changing sides with the paddle. He was a great believer that an important part of getting a fish to strike was in keeping him from knowing you were around.

His favorite lure in those early days was one he made at home. He cut a piece of flat, soft, white meat skin about one inch wide and five inches long. Then he cut a triangle wedge out of one end, starting at the outer tips and slanting inward to meet about halfway up. He then ran a hook through the uncut end, leaving the cut end as two streamers to follow behind. He used a line about three to four feet long, tied to a cane pole some ten to twelve feet long. As we moved around the edge where the grass and lily pads joined the open water, he would dip and flutter the bait on top with a little twisting motion of his wrist as he held the pole.

It was when the moon was rising that he thought the big bass would bite best. I learned to put absolute faith in this. The moon coming up had all the excitement of a curtain going up for a play. When I got the first glimpse of that white ball coming up over the hilltop in the east, making the shadows move and setting up a road of dancing lights on the water that came straight from the moon to me, my heart would beat faster in the knowledge that something very important was about to happen.

Papa and his friends carried on a soft chatter, usually telling about fishing experiences and swapping jokes, when the fish weren't biting. I listened, though I couldn't understand much of what they would talk about. One night, I remember Mr. Gibbs, the other man with us, told a story about Mutt and Jeff. They were in World War I and under heavy fire with shrapnel spraying left and right. Jeff gasped to Mutt as they retreated: "What color is blood?" Mutt replied, "yellow." Jeff then felt his backside and exclaimed in horror, "Oh, my God, I'm shot!" This got a big laugh from both Papa and our friend.

I didn't think to ask Papa later why this was so funny. But the next day in our third grade school class, the teacher told us that one of our classmates was sick and would be out of school and confined to bed for a long time. She suggested that we each write him a letter, and she explained that we should tell him something to cheer him up. She mentioned specifically that if we had heard a funny joke or story lately, to tell him about it. Later, each of us was called upon to read his letter, standing in front of the class. Mine, which included the Mutt and Jeff story of the night before, did not bring any response from the class. The teacher tactfully whispered to me that she would like to see me for a moment after school. Then she said, "Roy, about your letter; the story; did you think it was funny?" "No," I replied, "but the reason I thought sure it must be was because Papa and Mr. Gibbs, last night fishing, thought it was." "Well," she continued, "let this experience be a lesson. Don't ever tell any story you don't like yourself and don't laugh at a story someone else tells unless you really think it is funny." I then asked, "Mrs. Grambling, why did Papa think it was funny?" "Well," she said slowly, "sometime soon when just the two of you are together, you ask him that." I knew from the way she said it that she wanted our talk to end right there. I never brought up the matter again, to Papa or anyone else.

Up front on the lake, we were coming to a "point." This is what Papa always called a place where the grass or bonnets extended out to a peak from the more regular line of the curving edge of open water. "Easy, son," Papa admonished, "he sure ought to be here." He dropped the skin on top of a bonnet, then pulled it off with the flutter action of the pole. And he was there all right! Swash!

The night stood still. There was only the sound of the violent thrashing of the big bass when he felt the steel hook set in the gristle of the side of his huge mouth. Papa gave him the strength of the pole by raring back. The bend was so great that the butt end was almost pointing to where the fish was. As the big bass ran, Papa was trying to veer him out into open water by keeping the pole working against him. The big fellow tried to go deep for a mouthfull of the grass on the bottom which would help wrench the hook loose, but the pressure of the pole made him yield a little, and he shifted his strategy. He came up to the top twisting, thrashing away, in a lather of foam. Then Papa pressed the tip of his rod under the water to pull the big fish downward. A fish always has a better chance of freeing a hook from his mouth when he is thrashing on top than when he is swimming below the surface. Then the bass eased, tiring somewhat from his fight. This was Papa's signal to shift procedures. He pushed the butt end of the pole under his arm and back, starting a hand-over-hand pulling action and bringing the bass in toward us. Then I saw him—his mouth, rather. It was opened so wide you could have put a quart-size fruit jar in it. I couldn't see anything else of the fish, just that huge, gaping mouth and the pulsating red gills. He was just three feet away now and Papa was holding the pole tip and the line in his left hand, reaching to get his fingers under the gills with his right. Then the bass lunged downward under the boat, pulling the line from Papa's grasp. There was a moment of scramble in the boat when the pole must have slipped momentarily from Papa's grasp, but he recovered it firmly and in a few moments he and the bass were fighting it out again, this time with only half of the pole extended. Papa called to me, "Move the boat away from the grass out into the open water." I was so excited with the battle and the look of the bass's head in the moonlight that I had forgotten my boat-handling duties. I responded, though, and it wasn't long before the hand-over-hand pulling of the pole backward started again. This time the bass was spent and Papa expertly lifted the big fellow, all 13½ pounds of him, into the boat.

Papa, surveying his catch and almost out of breath, said, "You know, I thought for a while we had old Joe Nathan himself." Joe Nathan, he had explained before, was the one greatest, biggest, fightingest bass in Lake Jackson. He had hooked him, he thought, many times, but Joe was always able to get away. The big ones we actually landed that he thought were Joe all turned out to be Joe's "little brother," or "cousin," or "uncle."

At the end of every fishing trip, Papa always said, "Son, next time I believe we will get old Joe himself." And I believed him. It was a sad day for me when he told me the truth—like finding out the truth about Santa Claus. For a long time, you just know Santa cannot be and yet you want him to be so badly that you just stop asking questions about it so after the time of belief runs out you can stretch out a time of hope.

Papa brought up the subject once a few years later and put it in such a good way. We were talking out on the lake, and he said: "You know, there really is a Joe Nathan. No matter how big a fish you catch, there is always a bigger one you haven't caught. If you ever really got Joe, you might not want to keep coming back."

Over the years since, I have thought of Joe Nathan beyond any reference to fish or fishing. No matter what a good man does or how well he succeeds, he never achieves the perfection he wants. An author may write a good book, but he doesn't write his best book. The next one is always to be the best one. A lawyer may try a case with great skill, but a really good lawyer always knows he can do better on his next one. A man never catches old Joe Nathan, but he sure ought to keep trying, and keep feeling that he just might do it the next time.

7

☆ ☆ ☆ ☆ ☆

The Janes' Memorial Drive

SOMETIMES, I WONDER if we are not headed toward the final destruction of Florida's integrity by using up our natural beauty and advantages one by one. Much that we are doing to our land, sea, and air will surely destroy the character and wholeness of our state. At a rapid pace we are destroying irreplaceable values and calling it "success."

We would do better to preserve the broad bays dotted with mangrove islands—not convert all of them to narrow waterways between the cement seawalls of private housing projects.

We must stop the seemingly indiscriminate blocking out of the view of hammock lands, citrus groves, and wild range. We are often introduced to the beauty of our Florida countryside when a new road is built, opening up magnificent views of land and lake and sea. But, unfortunately, if we don't travel each new road soon after it is opened, we lose this thrill because the diversionary and concealing clutter of man moves right in.

We must better plan our cities and towns and highways, with the thought constantly in mind that people come here to be close to the miracles of the growth and beauty of the subtropics—not close for just a few last years while we tear out and cement over what's left—but close for their lifetime, our lifetime, and the lifetime of our children.

By no means is all lost.

There are countless quiet places in Florida, most of

them not on any suggested sightseeing tour, where you can feel a silence of history and the unspoiled watchfulness of nature. In such places, you can be within the landscape and a part of it, instead of watching it from some recommended place.

These should become hallowed and protected grounds.

One such spot, is near the City of Everglades, just a few miles north of the Tamiami Trail. The little town of Copeland lies there just to the west of State Road 29.

Uncounted millions of board feet of cypress went through Copeland's sawmill, which has been shut down for many years now. The company railroad used to wind northward into the swamp forests and haul out the giant virgin cypress. Now the tracks are gone but the roadbed has been turned into a narrow, unpaved, dead-end road, known bravely as the Janes' Memorial Drive, dedicated to the county by the Janes family long ago. They were in the tomato business.

Tomatoes were the earliest commercial product of that area. They were harvested and shipped by another railroad, the Deep Lake Railroad, of which hardly a trace remains. It ran south to the City of Everglades, where the tomatoes were taken by small boat to Key West, then by steamer to New York, where, in the days of Diamond Jim Brady, as an out-of-season delicacy, they brought up to $20 a crate at a time when $20 was two weeks pay for a bank clerk.

Behind the lumber mill site at Copeland, there are three old steam locomotives on short lengths of track. They were coated with a preservative which has kept them a dull, unrusted black, but wild green tropical vines now almost cover them.

When you drive up the Janes' Memorial Highway, you come to the largest stand of Royal Palm, growing wild, in Florida. They are not supposed to be indigenous to our land. How did they come to be there?

The most plausible answer is only theory: All the outcroppings of limestone in that area are solid with fossils from the bottom of what was once a shallow, tropical sea. When the Florida Peninsula slowly lifted out of the sea, thousands of years ago, this portion was the last to rise. A great storm once struck the Central American coast and tore the fertile seed pods from the palms and drove them far out to sea. Currents carried them for long weeks until, when they were off the Florida Coast, another tempest lifted them and carried them on huge waves inland to this place where topsoil had formed on the new land.

This could have happened a thousand times, with millions of the seeds, but only there, and in another place, far nearer the sea, at Royal Palm Hammock, did sufficient seeds root in close enough proximity to each other to form a viable colony. But the great stand of Royal Palms on either side of that hidden road, a few miles north of Copeland, is a thing of wild beauty and mystery, and an example of odds greater than in any sweepstakes.

This little road also penetrates the southern portion of the limited migratory pattern of the Florida panther. There are just a few of them left..They range, in season, from southeastern Manatee County down into the northern portion of Monroe County. Though they are one of our most protected mammals, as is true with many others, they do not breed well when a man moves too near.

It dismays me to think that since 1900, an average of 1.4 species of wild creature has become extinct each year. This means that in the past 65 years there were 92 creatures which have gone forever—creatures which nature took millions of years to create and equip for survival in the face of every hazard, except that single one she could not measure—the brain of man, with his avarice and hunger and indifference to the dignity of other forms of life.

The Florida panther is on the list to go. We don't know exactly when this will happen. Maybe ten years from now, or fifteen, or twenty, we will suddenly realize the last one has walked the earth and that we are just a little bit more alone on this planet.

No man then will ever again have the heart-stopping

experience of seeing, near a creek or canal, deeply imprinted into the moist sand, that great fresh pad mark, large as an inverted cup.

In April and May, millions of white spider lilies grow wild in the open spaces along the Janes' Memorial Drive. Each one is as fragile and lovely as the most expensive orchid in Manhattan.

All this is Nature's exquisite handiwork. But this is only one little pocket of history and of nature and that special brooding silence which can refresh the soul of man. I cannot think of any county in our state which does not have, far off the beaten track, a similar area of marshlands or wild range or piney woods.

And keep this in mind: There are silences across such land merely because it has not yet been practical commercially, to do anything but let it rest; silences that wait the eventual invasion which might come next year or in fifty years.

We should think ahead and plan to save these hidden places of our land. We should find ways with private and public funds, to buy them up for all the people of the generations to follow. This would be our state's great nature bank.

8

☆ ☆ ☆ ☆ ☆

Corbett vs. Mitchell

FIFTY-FIVE YEARS after the Read-Alston duel took place near Tallahassee, another famous "duel" was to take place in Jacksonville, although this one in retrospect had comic rather than tragic overtones.

By January 1894, Jacksonville's name had become headline news in many of the nation's newspapers. The unthinkable was going to happen. Jacksonville was scheduled to be the scene of a prizefight. James J. Corbett, the heavyweight champion of the world, was to defend his title against the well-known English boxer, Charles Mitchell.

When the fight was first announced in October 1893 by the Duval Athletic Club, there was considerable public and official opposition. Duncan U. Fletcher, later United States senator but then mayor of Jacksonville, said with much indignation: ". . . prize fighting tends to lawlessness. It is associated in the public mind with pickpockets, thieves, thugs, and blacklegs." The local clergy held a city-wide mass meeting to protest against the fight. The rector of St. John's Episcopal Church wrote open letters to the newspapers, saying that the spectators would only be "bad men and bad women." Another clergyman declared that it would "blunt the moral sentiments of our people and arouse the brutal instincts of humanity . . ." if the fight took place.

The Duval Athletic Club, however, refused to listen to the opposition and continued plans to hold the fight on

January 25, 1894, at the old fairgrounds, which had been leased from the Florida State Park Association. This is the present site of the beautiful new municipal stadium and was, at that time, just within the city limits. A prize purse of $20,000 had been made up for the principals and a check for half that amount had been sent to Richard K. Fox of New York, editor of the *Police Gazette* and a well-known sportsman.

There was at that time an anti-dueling law which was interpreted by state authorities to include prizefights. The issue became so heated that Governor Henry L. Mitchell (no relation to the fighter) was forced by public opinion to dispatch a special message forbidding the fight to take place. He declared his determination to save Florida from the disgrace of sanctioning a prizefight and vowed to use every power of the state and his office to prevent it. Many newspapers throughout the country began to take sides. The *New York World* compared football with boxing, condemning the latter as immoral, exceeding rough, and bloody.

Meanwhile, the contestants had arrived in Jacksonville; and "Gentleman Jim" Corbett went into training at Mayport while Mr. Mitchell established his training quarters at St. Augustine. The sponsors of the fight were trying to evade the law by calling it a "boxing match with five-ounce gloves" rather than a fight. The president of the Florida Park Association informed the sheriff of Duval County (Napoleon B. Broward, the future governor) that he should resist with force any attempt to enter the grounds, thus preventing the fight.

The sheriff favored the drastic measures of either jailing Corbett and Mitchell or forcibly taking over the fight arena to prevent the participants and ticket holders from entering. The Governor did not favor this course. His position was that if Corbett and Mitchell defied the law by staging the fight, they would have to suffer the consequences. This latter position was rationalized by holding that unless and until there actually was a fight, no crime had been committed. The adjutant-general went from Tallahassee to Jacksonville to confer with city officials on which course was to be pursued. The emotions of those who wanted the fight held and those who did not continued to heat up with equal force. Finally, after much deliberation, it was decided that martial law must be declared.

On January 17, the Gate City Rifles Company from Sanford was ordered to prepare to march to Jacksonville. The Second Battalion of state troops was also alerted. The steam in Jacksonville's boiler became hotter by the hour.

Lillian Lewis, a popular actress of the day, announced that she would be present at the fight "if she should prove the only woman within 100 miles of the spot." In a day when such action was unthinkable and scandalous for even an actress, it was necessary for her manager to issue an immediate retraction to the effect that "Miss Lewis has no desire to see any kind of prize fight and she knows ladies do not and cannot attend such exhibitions." Even so, Miss Lewis placed a $1,200 bet on Mitchell.

Two days before the fight, the state militia marched into the city. As they paraded through the crowded streets, promoters of the fight hissed and booed, and some of them even threw sand and rocks at the troops.

Meanwhile, the Duval Athletic Club decided to play its trump card. It appealed for an injunction restraining the sheriff from invading club property for the purpose of interfering with the "proposed scientific glove contest." The case was before Circuit Judge Rhydon M. Call and was argued for the club by Colonel A. W. Cockrell, one of the state's most prominent lawyers, supported by a nationally-famous lawyer imported from St. Louis. The state attorney general came over from Tallahassee and, with the state's attorney, argued the case for the state. The hearing lasted until the day before the fight and was decided in favor of the club. So the injunction issued.

The day of the fight dawned dismally. Rain poured in

torrents and carriages churned the mud until the streets were almost impassable. Jacksonville was jammed with crowds and curiosity seekers. It had been impossible to get hotel or boarding room accommodations for weeks before the fight because of the incredibly strong demand. Hotel Everett on Bay Street, the Windsor Hotel, the Duval Hotel, and the St. James were filled to overflowing with sportsmen and gamblers who had come from as far away as New York and Chicago for the event. It was the largest crowd ever assembled in Jacksonville for an event of any kind. The publicity brought on by all the controversy had made the event assume a degree of prominence far beyond the bounds of reality. A simple desire to go had been transformed into a fierce demand by thousands.

The fight was scheduled to begin about 2 o'clock in the afternoon; but by 11 o'clock, the crowd had begun to gather at the fairgrounds. All the hacks and rattletrap conveyances in the city were pressed into service and were hitched behind nags, horses, and mules. The going cost of transportation was a dollar per person from town to ringside. Many persons walked to the fairgrounds, others sailed upriver in excursion boats, and many rode horseback. By noon, the seats had begun to fill rapidly. The tickets were sold for $10 to $25 each, and the house was sold out long before the starting time. The fight promoters, certain the fight would be held, had sent the sheriff a $25 ringside seat, but it was not used.

It was a boisterous crowd of "sporting" men which had gathered around the ring and there were "few present who did not have something in the shape of a flask in their hip pockets, or a basket of beer within easy reach."

A sensation was created when, just before the fight began, a woman, dressed in men's clothes, entered and took a seat. She was (though this was not admitted) easily recognized by many of the prominent men present as Clara Desplaines, owner of the most famous brothel in Kansas City.

"Gentleman Jim," defending the title for the United States, was the first to enter the ring. He and Mitchell had arrived in the city earlier and their respective tents had been set up at opposite ends of the fairgrounds. The crowd became impatient waiting for Mitchell to appear. Steve Brodie, of Brooklyn Bridge athletic fame, was one of the spectators. When some fellow hopped up and in a loud voice cried out that he would bet a thousand head of cattle on Corbett, another shouted back, "Bring on your cattle. Mitchell can knock them out too!"

Mitchell finally appeared, wearing a pair of brightly colored jerseys clasped about the ankles with black straps. The two men faced each other across the ring after their final instructions. The gong rang for the first round.

The fight was "short and sweet"—an anticlimax after such a build up. Corbett knocked Mitchell out in the third round and "Gentleman Jim" thus retained his title as heavyweight champion of the world.

The two boxers were arrested after the fight, and as soon as Mitchell had been revived both were charged with committing a misdemeanor. They posted bonds and left the following day for the North. Trials were scheduled for February.

Corbett appeared for trial. The fever over boxing had subsided by then and a jury of six men, four whites and two Negroes, deliberated for 15 minutes before bringing in a verdict of "not guilty." The case against Mitchell was then dropped.

What a ruckus over a prize fight! Why, today we are subjected to more violence than that in a single thirty second television commercial about acid indigestion.

Courtesy of University of Florida Press

9

☆ ☆ ☆ ☆ ☆

Napoleon Bonaparte Broward and His Three Friends

INTRODUCTORY

I HAVE THE privilege of serving as an elector of "The Hall of Fame of Great Americans" (oldest and most prestigious of all the halls of fame) established at New York University. This group has a rule that no one who has not been dead for twenty-five years or more is eligible for election. The reasons for this are primarily that it takes the passage of time for the elements and events of a human life to come into a good focus; and further, time is required to avoid the pressures of campaigns waged for or against nominees by emotionally motivated contemporaries.

Applying this rule, it is my own assessment that Napoleon Bonaparte Broward was Florida's greatest governor. When a political leader's name comes to be associated with his time in the minds of people, this alone is an indication of greatness; and historians commonly refer to the period of Broward's term as the governor of Florida, as the "Broward Era."

The qualities that to me are of most importance in judging a political leader are: (1) His "integrity;" and I use the term in its broadest sense of "wholeness" and the reflection of a leader's faithfulness to the public interest

119

in all actions he takes; (2) his ability to make tough decisions; (3) his administrative competence to get his decisions implemented; and (4) his "style," "charisma," or whatever one may call those personal qualities that enable a man to have mass appeal. Leaders can come up short on some of these and still do a good job but to Broward, more than to any other, I would give a very high grade on all four.

While I will take from his whole life with a few broad dips, I do not intend this to be a biographical synopsis. I want to tell here the story of the pre-Spanish-American War experiences which all came before Broward took on the governorship.

EARLY LIFE

Two influences, over neither of which Napoleon Broward had any control, deeply affected his life. First of all there was the Civil War which was ending when he was a very young child. The Broward family had for generations been one of social distinction, substantial wealth, high educational standards, political influence, and universal respect. They lived in great homes with large libraries and had the services of many slaves. The grandfather, John Broward, was a successful soldier, planter, and politician who exerted a strong influence throughout Northeast Florida where he chose to settle before the Florida territory was acquired by the United States. He raised ten children in big houses and on lands mostly obtained under Spanish grants. One of these children was the first Napoleon Bonaparte Broward, who also became a large, influential, land and slave owner of Duval County, Florida. He was born in 1829 and in 1851 married Mary Dorcas Parsons from a prominent family in New Hampshire. There were eight children born to this union and the names given them speak for the dash and spirit of a strong father and mother: Josephine, Napoleon, Montcalm, Mary Dorcas, Emily, Osceola, Hortense, and California.

It is with this latter Napoleon that this piece is concerned. While born to wealth and the style of aristocracy in 1857, he was not destined to grow up in the manner born because the war destroyed the family economic base. His father had a most difficult time trying to provide for his large family during the depressed postwar period. The educational opportunities and social advantages which would have come to young Napoleon under normal circumstances became impossible. The family became divided, and the father had to accept inconspicuous employment at times in Jacksonville simply to make ends meet.

Thus young Napoleon, while deeply aware of his heritage and strongly influenced by it, was confronted with the necessity of making his own way early in life. This involved toughening, hard work on his grandfather's farm which gave him an unusually strong body to go with his equally strong spirit and determination.

He left school in 1875 to go to work on an uncle's steamboat and in this decision there surfaced a reflection of the second great influence on his early life—the St. Johns River. This beautiful and unique river, long an important artery of commerce, rises deep in Central Florida and flows north to Jacksonville where it moves on out to join the Atlantic Ocean.

Traffic on the St. Johns in those days was providing much of the burgeoning strength of the Jacksonville economy. Substantial quantities of freight and passengers moved up and down, to and from the lesser ports on its banks. The river was young Napoleon's friend. He lived on it, moved on it, in all kinds of boats and weather. He knew it intimately, its channels, its bars, its bounty, and those who navigated it—the rough, tough, good and bad. After working several months, he quit and went back to school staying with a Captain Summers, who was a lighthouse keeper living alone in his lighthouse which stood out into the river about 200 yards from Dames Point. This experience, of course, drew Napoleon still closer to shipping and the sea, as on off hours he listened to the tales of the Captain and his friends. He kept up with his studies well in this association.

The following summer, after school closed, Broward began a period of working travel, shipping out on various freight carrying vessels that moved to ports in far off parts of the world. Ultimately his work always brought him back to Jacksonville where he became involved in the water shipping business in several capacities. He had acquired full competence as a seaman and navigator, wearing easily the title of "Captain." Broward also engaged in other business enterprises, and became a strikingly handsome, popular, respected business leader of Jacksonville.

The sheriff of Duval County made a serious mistake in handling a criminal matter and Florida Governor Edward A. Perry asked for his resignation. The local Democratic Committee recommended that Broward be appointed to fill the vacancy. The *Florida Times-Union* of Jacksonville endorsed him as a "man possessed of four prerequisites—integrity, honesty, courage, and above all, absolute sobriety."

When the Governor made the appointment, the *Times-Union* was quick to praise the action as "one of the very best that has ever been made in Duval County."

Broward's performance was first rate. He was a fearless law and order man, dealing with many difficult circumstances skillfully and effectively. His reputation grew. But his politics also became complicated by the great political upheavals of that time and in 1888 Broward, as the Democratic nominee, was opposed by a Republican named Moody, and was defeated in the general election. However, a technicality developed over the qualifications of the sheriff-elect to take the office and the Supreme Court ruled that he was not eligible. In the aftermath of this squabble Governor Francis P. Fleming reappointed Broward.

Following this Broward became identified more closely with city and state politics and throughout the state he became known as a fearless, trustworthy, and glamorous fighter for reform. It became clear that he was determined to help the average citizen to get a better opportunity and to suppress what he sensed was the growing power of a few strong vested interests which were exploiting the people of the state and their natural resources. His target became particularly the railroads, and he strongly advocated a state railroad commission to help eliminate railroad and corporate abuses. His strong supporter, the Florida *Times-Union,* portending things to come, was now characterizing him as "a holy terror."

Just when it appeared that Broward was headed for a statewide political effort, events developed that diverted his interests and placed his entire future in serious jeopardy.

THE FILIBUSTERS

Broward had a growing family by 1895, a second wife and three daughters. A fine, new house he had long intended to build was ready and occupied in March of that year. It was one of Jacksonville's first to have electric lights in every room. Appropriately, the floors and woodwork were made of Honduras mahogany which had been salvaged from a wrecked steamer and saved for this use.

As his business interests developed successfully, he always continued his interest in the sea, the river, and waterborne commerce. With his brother, Montcalm, and George DeCottes he raised $40,000 with which the three built to their own specifications "a powerful seagoing tug." The owners intended to take advantage of the fast growing towing and salvage business developing all along the east coast and also to carry passengers to and from Nassau and

other ports in the Bahamas. At a loss for an appropriate
name, someone suggested that they give this privilege to
the highest bidder. After an exciting auction with spirited
bids, Decottes won on a bid of $80.00 and gave to the new
ship the name, the *Three Friends*.

At the launching a happy group of prominent Jacksonville friends gathered. Broward, back in his favorite role,
black coat glistening and white captain's cap correct and
immaculate, gave the order for the ship to be freed. His
daughter, Hortense, smashed a bottle of wine on the bow,
all those present cheered loudly, a great chorus of whistles
screeched and bellowed from other ships all over the harbor, and the *Three Friends* slid down the ways to begin

a life's voyage destined to be tumultuous and precarious, not only for herself, but for her owners, and especially for her gallant captain, Napoleon Bonaparte Broward.

Already, the world was becoming jittery over insurrection brewing in Cuba. Spain's control of the beautiful island and its exciting and excitable people was eroding rapidly, though the Spaniards desperately were pretending this was not the case. The revolutionaries were developing greater and greater sympathy and encouragement from citizens of the United States and this was especially the case with former Cubans residing along the Atlantic Coast and around Tampa.

Filibustering activity to get arms and supplies to the revolutionaries was growing rapidly in Florida. The short distance of 90 miles that separated Florida from Cuba, over the years had encouraged intimate knowledge and personal ties. Besides, the coast of Florida, especially that nearest Cuba, was made up of thousands of inlets, mangrove islands, channels, and coves, affording unlimited opportunities for avoiding detection and capture by smugglers moving in or out.

The mangrove of Southern Florida's tidal shores is a bushy tree of unusual characteristics. The average height of a mature tree is around twenty feet and the diameter varies from four to six inches. A single tree develops a large network of adventitious roots which arch out and downward into the mud where they continue to grow. This mass catches silt and mud brought in from the sea on the tides and thus develops in due course a solid terrain which will support vegetation seeded from inland forests. It bears as fruit a conical berry about one inch long, which germinates the seed. The seedling becomes dartlike and grows to be between six and twelve inches long by the time it is released. Upon separation the heavy end lodges securely in the mud and the upper part sends out immediately lush leafy shoots. These tough soil-building trees have been extremely important in land growth around the Keys and flatlands of both of Florida's southern coasts. They grow out into the water in every conceivable kind of pattern and form the irregular borders of innumerable canals and inlets. There is a sameness of appearance that is extremely treacherous for the navigator, and from Florida's earliest days they have afforded almost impenetrable sanctuaries for fugitives from the law.

The United States was insisting in its diplomatic relations with Spain that it was doing everything possible to prevent the supply of American arms to the insurrectionists. Spain felt otherwise, and charged (correctly) that a very large percentage of all the supplies getting to those resisting Spanish authority in Cuba was coming directly from the United States, mostly through smuggling activity operating out of Florida. President Grover Cleveland responded with more and more vigorous efforts to stop this illegal traffic.

Large numbers of personnel, gunboats, and other armed vessels were employed to oversee, detect, and prevent violations of rigid laws against filibustering activities. But, the game of hide and seek continued to be won by the hiders. They knew the Florida waters better than the "Feds," and, importantly too, they knew that public sentiment was heavily on their side and would furnish aid in many forms for their operations.

As the *Three Friends* was being fitted out, Broward was keenly aware of the march of events. He was strongly for the insurrectionists in his feelings and even expressed the hope that the Congress of the United States would formally recognize and sanction the free Cuba movement. He was itching to get involved, evidently feeling that the time had come when all his maritime experience and leadership could be utilized in a thrilling and profitable fight to aid a noble people to overcome evil oppression.

But Broward was determined to obey the law, and the maiden voyage of the *Three Friends* in mid-January 1896 was destined for Nassau with a cargo of flour and fertilizer.

When she returned, however, additional freight charters did not materialize nor was there need for salvage services. So Broward had reason to be discouraged, but not for long.

There was a large Cuban colony in Jacksonville which had become organized to promote a free Cuba. The leader of the group was J. A. Huau, a cigar maker, who was also a close friend of Broward's. Broward knew that Huau's group was involved in making numerous shipments of Cuban recruits and supplies from Florida ports to Cuba without detection, and when Huau contacted Broward to enlist his help Broward agreed to a plan he both liked and felt would meet the letter of the law. He would take the recruits, if they would sign on as regular passengers, and munitions if they were loaded on the *Three Friends* at sea beyond the three-mile limit.

Then there was developed a very complicated arrangement in a meeting held in the Huau Cigar Factory. The owners of the *Three Friends* agreed to transport a group of Cuban patriots to be under the command of a Cuban General, Enrique Colasso, who at that time was hiding in the home of a friend in Tampa, and a load of munitions which would be transferred from the schooner, *Stephen R. Mallory,* then at Cedar Key. Sixty-five of Colasso's men were on another schooner, the *Ardell.* Now, to bring this all off: (1) Colasso was to come secretly to Jacksonville from Tampa; (2) the *Mallory* would rendezvous with the *Three Friends* at the mouth of Caesar's Creek (on the east coast, south of Miami and; (3) the *Ardell* would bring the sixty-five recruits for transfer in the Florida Keys near Hawk Channel. Thus loaded, the *Three Friends* would proceed to Cuba and unload.

All these plans were placed in jeopardy by violent occurrences. A part of what would have been the *Mallory's* cargo was intercepted at Tampa. There were many large boxes marked "groceries." Unopened, these were sent to a consignee at Jacksonville. There they were hidden, then stealthily put aboard the *Three Friends.* General Colasso was regarded as a very special prize to be taken by the United States and his location in Tampa was detected there before he could leave for Jacksonville. He left his hiding place in a carriage with several of his staff, and U.S. detectives were in close pursuit. At a point previously agreed upon, the carriage stopped and the General and all but one of his staff got out and ran for cover. The pursuing officers did not detect this but soon afterward caught up with the carriage in which they thought the General was still riding. The occupant disguised now as Colasso, upon arrival at Port Tampa quickly boarded a ship which departed in moments destined for Key West, but not before the confident pursuers were taken aboard also. In the meantime, the real General Colasso, by plan, had been picked up and driven to Plant City where he boarded a train which transported him safely to Jacksonville.

The *Three Friends* was now ready to complete its preparations to sail. She quietly loaded the "groceries" which included two rapid fire cannons, 500 pounds of dynamite, 3,000 Winchester rifles, 500 machetes, 1,000,000 repriming caps, 500 pounds of sulfur, and large quantities of other munitions, clothing, and medicines. Broward told inspectors that he was headed for Palm Beach, and pulled away from the wharf with his full crew. Three miles from Jacksonville he picked up General Colasso and two of his aides. Also another large launch was put aboard and two iron surf boats to be used for unloading cargo, and the order was then given to proceed south under full speed.

By dawn they were far away, a new coat of steel gray had replaced her usual white coat of paint, and the *Three Friends* now bore the name, *The Ox*. As they worked their way down the coast of Florida, they were constantly fearful of interception and encountered some rough seas; but on the morning of the thirteenth they entered the channel off Cape Florida and sighted the *Mallory* anchored near Elliotts Key. A rendezvous was arranged for the following morning near Indian Key, where Broward thought the transfer of supplies could be effected. Morning brought an even rougher sea with both vessels rolling and pitching furiously but the transfer was accomplished after long and difficult work.

The problem then became how to find the *Ardell*. After much searching the vessel was contacted and the job of transferring the sixty-five Cubans patriots to the *Three Friends* was completed.

Captain Broward then with his cargo complete set his course due south for a point off the coast of Cuba where he expected to arrive in a matter of a few hours. He told all of the recruits to keep carefully out of view until dark and they would be landed before dawn.

What a night this turned out to be! First they were expecting to be met by a small schooner which ordinarily escorted filibusters in for unloadings, and no schooner showed up. In previous planning they had arranged to have aboard an experienced Cuban pilot named Santos who was to take charge of the navigation when the shore was being approached. Santos took charge, as agreed, with the *Three Friends* rolling and pitching heavily in a strong wind and a heavy rain that almost obscured all vision. Santos was determined that the course should be south and Broward was certain the course should be southwest and ordered him to change. Santos yielded but thirty minutes later he turned south again. Violent arguments ensued but this time Broward yielded to the pilot. Still fearful of Santos's seamanship Broward called for depth soundings, and when he was advised there was only twenty-four feet, he quickly ordered full speed astern to avoid the danger of being grounded. Before the forward movement could be checked adequately the bow hit the shallow breakers, but the measures taken prevented grounding. Then Santos announced that they had arrived at the right place to unload and the anchor was lowered.

While still doubting Santos's judgment, Broward gave the order to unload. A lifeboat containing six of the

Cubans started for the beach to reconnoiter. Before getting any report back Santos ordered other boats loaded and launched. Fifteen Cubans were put in each boat between cases of munition and supplies and rowed ashore. Minutes later it was learned that they had anchored very near a Spanish town that no one could identify. It was protected by a fort only a hundred yards off their starboard side. Meantime on the shore the first boat load of scouts, realizing that they were precariously deposited right in front of the enemy's guns on the fort, ran for hiding places in the nearby brush. The other boats that were coming in ran into various obstacles. One was wrecked on a reef. Three were swamped when they hit the beach. A wild scramble then developed to bury the munitions on the beach before their presence was detected. General Colasso, still aboard the *Three Friends,* ordered one of his subordinates to take one of the remaining lifeboats ashore and bring back the Cubans as quickly as possible. Then he changed his mind and decided to wait until the next night and try another landing of reinforcements. Broward, encouraged by the still silent fort, thought they could take the little town by surprise and capture it if they proceeded to complete a landing. Though Colasso agreed to this, Broward could not get volunteers from his own crew members to undertake it.

It was about this time that the Spaniards on shore woke up and jumped into action. First a search light from a Spanish gunboat nearby flooded the beach and lighted up all the furious digging and burying activity going on there. Then bullets started spraying the beach. Cuban patriot guns soon put out the light with some well aimed fire, lessening briefly their danger. Broward, searching the sea now to determine what else might be in the vicinity, discovered a large gunboat off the port side about one mile away. Flares from the gunboats were now lighting up the whole scene. Several shells from the small gunboat exploded very close to the *Three Friends* rocking the ship severely. Broward ordered his men on board: "Do not use your guns! The fire will attract [the] large gunboat. . . . Get your axes and lie under the bulwarks. If this small gunboat attempts to board us, use them!" Broward further said, "I promised the sailors that I would not leave them on the beach. Rather than do it, if capture is imminent, I will beach . . . and we will all fight together."

But moments later two of the landing boats from shore pulled alongside. As the men were being pulled aboard a shell exploded some fifty feet away The Captain then shouted to secure the boats to the davits, cut the anchor cable, and full speed ahead. A real race was on. The men and Broward well knew that if they did not win it they would be taken and summarily shot by the Spaniards. The *Three Friends* was running a little north of east almost parallel with the Cuban coastline. The Spanish vessel was headed east on a course that would cross the bow of Broward's vessel at very close range. In another few minutes the Spanish vessel could fire point blank at the *Three Friends*. Realizing how precarious the situation was, Broward told his first mate to "line all the men on the port side and have them ready to get in the boats. I shall run into him as we are now moving and I believe that both boats will be sunk in the collision." "What then Captain," the mate asked. "We will have the advantage," said Broward, "of having our men ready."

At this point, Broward remembered that he had brought aboard a supply of very fine fat pine that could give his furnaces very quick and intense heat in an emergency. He ordered the furnaces filled with this material and they soon glowed red hot. At the same time the fat caused billows of very dark smoke to pour out the stack. Then he turned the *Three Friends* sharply and headed west, with the wind blowing the smoke back eastward into the bay. In the dimness the Spanish believed that the *Three Friends* had doubled back on her course so they turned toward the bay though Broward had turned north to the open sea. In the night and the rain the *Three Friends* was soon out of sight and well on her course to Key West where she landed by morning and got rid of her remaining cargo.

It was around noon on Sunday, March 22, when the *Three Friends* steamed back into the port of Jacksonville. With a new coat of white and her true name now proudly in place she showed no wear and tear from her nightmarish experience off the coast of Cuba. Captain Broward, in an immaculate white uniform, walked briskly and confidently to the surrey in which Mrs. Broward awaited his return.

He had much to tell his family. The press and authorities anxiously awaited what he would tell them too. Since the word of the filibustering voyage had beat him back to Jacksonville he had to have answers. He spoke partially in jest knowing that public sentiment was on his side. In answer to some questions he asked questions himself, jovially disclaiming knowledge of filibustering activities and referring to his operations up and down the east coast of Florida and on to Key West. This seemed to satisfy almost everyone except the American and Spanish authorities.

No government action was taken based upon the ill-fated Cuban trip but the U.S. marshal at Jacksonville was directed from Washington to "require the master of the *Three Friends* . . . to give a bond that he will not engage in any enterprise in contravention of international law." To this was added this statement: "The Department is of the opinion that the facts in the case do warrant the seizure or libeling of the vessel." That same day the local collector of customs received a wire from the Secretary of the Treasury, forbidding the *Three Friends* to leave the St. Johns River until further notice and Captain Kilgore of the U.S. Cutter *Boutwell*, moved his ship close to the *Three Friends* and trained its guns on her.

Broward was well aware that his operations were under

close and unfriendly scrutiny but he did not know of Kilgore's latest action and at daybreak the next morning the *Three Friends* quietly and nonchalantly moved out into the channel and headed toward the Atlantic. Soon the *Boutwell* was following close behind. Notwithstanding the surveillance a stop was made, and the crew commenced loading arms and ammunition. A launch also brought guns from shore to Broward's ship which anchored in midstream. Then Broward steamed back to Jacksonville anchoring at the ship's regular dock, with the cutter still close behind.

Broward, upon hearing further about the directions from Washington, protested, claiming he was about to make a peaceful trip to Key West. Inspections followed and the crates aboard were found carefully marked "ship stores." Without opening any of them the inspector reported that the expected trip was not disclosed to be a "military expedition" and the *Three Friends* was then free to go on its way. Broward was personally confronted by the Spanish consul. In the company of several others also, Broward was asked about his cargo. He replied very calmly and matter of factly, "I've got one hundred twenty tons of coal and a whole boatload of arms and ammunition for Key West." The consul was astounded at this unexpected frankness and asked, "What for do you have so much coal, Captain?" Someone else then said there was a good market for selling coal in Key West, to which the Spaniard responded, "I did not hear he sold coal when he go to Key West before." Then he added as an afterthought: "Queer country. Everybody know where you go, but nobody can testify."

The *Three Friends* got underway with clearance from Washington but followed again by the *Boutwell*. During the night Broward picked up a load of Cuban patriots from other vessels by prearrangements without detection and before dawn the *Boutwell* had lost trace of her and turned back to Jacksonville.

Later Broward delivered his cargo at another key, not Key West, because as Broward explained he had to divert because of bad weather. He further claimed that he had picked up two barges belonging to Henry Flagler, but when he arrived back in Jacksonville no barges were in tow.

There followed many similar secret movements with the able Captain Broward always the winner and the Spanish and American authorities alike continually frustrated. After every exploit Broward would come back to Jacksonville vowing that he had no plans for any further voyages. Then the *Three Friends* would pull one of its disappearing acts again and the people would be thrilled later to learn of new ways the authorities had been outmaneuvered.

Once the revenue cutter *Winona* was chasing the filibuster steamer *City of Key West* which sought to hide in a small cove. There she was stopped and boarded by Navy officers who found many irregularities including nearly 500 cases of ammunition. The control of the ship was taken over by *Winona* officers and she was headed back to Key West. On the way, by chance, a lookout detected a steamer lying anchored near Knight Key. A small boat was lowered from the anchored vessel but quickly returned when it got a signal of warning from a regular crew member of the *Key West*. Unable to escape, the vessel was boarded by the authorities who had command of the *Key West* and it was discovered to be the *Three Friends,* whose cargo included a small quantity of ammunition. Captain Broward hotly contested orders to proceed to Key West, but could not avoid doing so. There, however, it was found that the cargo did not fall within the limits prohibited by law and the *Three Friends* was free again to pursue its devious course.

A few hours out of Key West, the *Three Friends* saw a three-masted warship they thought was a Spanish vessel. Broward sought to escape but was hotly pursued by what turned out to be the U.S.S. *Raleigh*. The *Raleigh* in turn sought the help of the U.S.S. *Maine* which was anchored near Key West. But, the *Three Friends,* before the *Raleigh* could close in, made a sharp left turn entering water protected by narrow reefs. Knowing that it could not follow the big ship gave up the idea of chase.

When the *Three Friends* next steamed into Fernandina, north of Jacksonville, her officers would not reveal the names of any foreign ports she had visited and without such a showing the health authorities ordered the vessel completely sterilized. Three days later she returned home to Jacksonville.

Broward returned the conquering hero, not the tarnished outlaw. Coming up the river the other vessels added to the riotous welcome-back-home of the *Three Friends*. The *Times-Union* reported that flags were "flying proudly in the breeze . . . every craft that could whistle, from a Naptha up to a Clyde Line and every mill along the shore from Mayport to the City, welcomed the boat." The shrill whistle of the *Three Friends* sounded "like a cunarder." The now famous little vessel was escorted in with the highest honors. Mrs. Broward's carriage was waiting for the Captain as usual, but this time it had been decorated with red, white, and blue bunting. As Broward came down the gangplank he was greeted warmly by a committee of high city officials, and there followed a parade through the heart of the city with thousands lining the way to cheer the hero's return.

America seemed certain now to be headed toward war with Spain. Cleveland's further efforts to maintain neutrality were no more effective than a lone cowboy out in front facing a stampeding herd of cattle commanding it to stop. The Spanish were vigorously protesting filibustering activity but every protest seemed to stir more public approval of the deed. The Spanish further offered a reward of $25,000 for the capture of any filibuster captain, dead or alive, so a substantial price was on Broward's head.

Broward and his partners had the hull of the *Three Friends* improved in a dry dock servicing operation and he had come back to Jacksonville after a brief respite in Georgia with his family. He was reluctant to say when his next trip would occur or its destination. With rumors strong that much ammunition was in the city destined for Cuba, many assumed that it would be Broward and his *Three Friends* who would take it there. One of Broward's men let out the word that the *Three Friends* planned to go to a key near Key West where it would seek to salvage a Mexican tug that had been sunk. This sounded like a typical Broward effort to make a false trail, with work going on all night to finish the overhaul work and load the *Three Friends* with what was reported to be hundreds of oblong boxes. The crew also had some new surf boats placed aboard, which a newspaper reported would be used to help raise the tug. When loading was complete the vessel sailed but was stopped at Mayport by Broward's old antagonist, the *Boutwell*. Though Broward protested vehemently, Captain Kilgore insisted that the *Three Friends* return to Jacksonville for an inspection. There, the customs collector joined in the search which revealed no more than a regular and normal cargo. This brought a release of the *Three Friends* from custody but Kilgore was ordered again to follow her wherever she went. But Broward decided not to go anywhere. More rumors spread regarding new cargo loadings of the *Three Friends* and more inspections followed with no offending cargo found. Finally, the *Three Friends* sailed without Broward. But, shortly before, other ships in the harbor were loaded with munitions and had sailed unnoticed; all eyes were riveted on the *Three Friends*. Outside the three-mile limit the cargoes were transferred to the *Three Friends* and she proceeded unmolested to Pinar Del Rio where she delivered seventy-five patriots, some American and Russian free lance soldiers, 465,000 rounds of ammunition, 1,000 rifles, one dynamite gun, 2,000 pounds of dynamite,

1,000 machetes, and a large supply of clothes and medicines. Coming back via Key West the vessel was placed in quarantine because of her foreign exposure and when she returned to Fernandina the United States Treasury Department ordered the ship detained for a full investigation as to her recent operation. Other charges followed encouraged by charges made by the Spanish, bond was required, and the use of the vessel was severely restricted. Broward was charged both with violations of international law and violations of the U.S. neutrality laws. He seemed clear on the former but not on the latter.

In the meantime he seemed determined to act in defiance of the law. By putting out a rumor in Jacksonville that he would use a vessel named the *Commodore* for his next expedition, he diverted the attention of those who were seeking to prevent filibustering from the *Three Friends* to a careful watch of the *Commodore*. To heighten suspicion a sign was put up by the *Commodore* gangplank reading "positively no admittance." This was the cover needed and the *Three Friends* quietly moved up to Fernandina where she took on another load of Cubans and munitions and put out to sea. The trip was handicapped by severe weather—rain and fog—as she approached the shores of Cuba. Protected by the fog a small Spanish gunboat specially alerted to search out and sink the *Three Friends,* because of her renown as a successful filibusterer, moved in close and opened fire for what her commander thought would be a sure kill. The second shot landed so close that the whole vessel was awash from the waves. The *Three Friends* took a sharp turn for the open sea. A gun mounted on her bow quickly returned fire and one of its shells scored a hit, crippling the pursuer. By this time, though, help was rushing in to give chase. But again the *Three Friends* was more skillfully navigated and made it into the Keys and safety. The cargo was unloaded on an uninhabited nearby key for later pick up and delivery.

There followed months of more charges and litigation.

Also, moving into the White House succeeding Cleveland was President William McKinley who was backed strongly by the young Republicans led by Theodore Roosevelt who were ready now for war.

Litigation in the Supreme Court of the United States resulted in a ruling against Broward and his fellow fili-busters, but the decision was never enforced in a manner adverse to the *Three Friends* or Broward, and they continued to ply the coast looking for wrecks, though now carrying aboard a U.S. marshal!

Most historians now concede that the Spanish-American War would never have happened had young William Randolph Hearst not deliberately goaded the country into wanting it through the use of the rankest kind of irrespon-sible journalism. Frederick Remington, then a Hearst man in Havana, at one pre-war point sent this telegram to his boss:

> Everything is quiet. There is no trouble here. There will be no war. I wish to return."
>
> > (Signed)   "Remington

This was Hearst's reply:

> "Please remain. You furnish the pictures and I'll furnish the war."

And he did. By lurid reports far out of the bounds of truth, by invented atrocities, by sensation mongering, the American people were maneuvered not into a position of tolerating war, but of wanting it to avenge the country's national honor.

But the war is another story.

So is the later service of Napoleon B. Broward, as Florida's nineteenth governor.

As for the *Three Friends,* as the reader may have surmised, she lived out her charmed life in a peaceful old age, rotting away in the mud on a bank of the St. Johns. The ship's ghosts however, which have hovered around, were numerous, and aggressive in the tall tales of adventure they have had to tell.

10

☆ ☆ ☆ ☆ ☆

Mama and the Outlaw Watson

THE TIME AND storm scarred little sloop was pitching and rolling in the black night, and the rain kept coming down in gusts and sheets. Mama, clutching her knees that were covered by her full length, homemade skirt, was shivering as much from fear as from the wet cold. She was in a corner of the deck with packing boxes right and left, close to where the man was handling the tiller. The fact that she was the only girl on board with four men did not worry her. Her stomach, on the verge of revolt, was of much more concern.

The pilot was talking with his voice raised a notch or two over the sound of the sea. "So you are going to Chokoloskee. Good Lord girl, do you know how to shoot?" "Shoot what?" Mama asked. "There's no telling," he said, "that's bad country. Bad snakes, bad men. And when you run into either one of them, if you don't kill him, sure as hell he will kill you!"

* * * * *

Mama was a nineteen year old girl in that year of 1898. Now she is ninety-one and enjoying good health. Her maiden name was Mattie Brandon. Her father was Thomas Brandon, a farmer, and her great grandfather was Thomas Jones, the owner and builder of Greenwood, magnificent southern mansion at Thomasville Georgia. Greenwood is now owned by John Hay Whitney. Mama

was the first of five children and got her early education in Thomasville, near the farm on which she was
born. After attending a school in Thomasville, she matric-
ulated in the Women's State College of Georgia at Mil-
ledgeville and two years later she was ready to prepare for
and take the Florida state teacher examination. This required two months special training in Tallahassee, where
she came to know many other girls her age from all over
the state.

After passing the examination and getting her license,
upon the encouragement of a friend, she accepted a position to teach in a county school in the woods near Alva, a
community on the Caloosahatchee River about sixteen
miles upstream from Ft. Myers. Her salary was $40 per
month, out of which she paid her board. To get there, she
went by train as far as Punta Gorda, then by riverboat on
to Ft. Myers.

The county superintendent took her to Alva in his
buggy, where she found another ride waiting to take her
to her first schoolhouse—a crude, one-room, thatched-roof
structure that trembled and rattled in the wind. There
were no supplies—just a desk made from shipping boxes
for the teacher and homemade, no-back benches for students. There were no books to teach from except the few
that the teacher had brought with her. The need for books
was partly met when the children, responding to their
teacher's request, brought whatever books they could find
at home. It was quite a wide assortment, and with these
the teacher commenced her work of educating a dozen or
so boys and girls of ages ranging from six to sixteen who
seemed to come and go whenever it pleased them.

After two months, one day during a high wind the roof
on the schoolhouse blew away and the rain poured in without hindrance. The superintendent came from Ft. Myers
and, there being no other place for the school to go,
it was agreed that Mama would be forced to discontinue
her work there.

Before she could complete her plans to return home to North Florida, the superintendent came back and, evidently recognizing that Mama's fine qualities were mixed with considerable gullibility, requested her to go to the island community of Chokoloskee, farther south in the Ten Thousand Islands, and there resume teaching. Something had happened to the previous teacher there, so he convinced Mama that she should go and serve the remaining four months of the current term. She did not know it, but Chokoloskee then was so remote that few people ever seriously considered going there; that is, for good and lawful reasons.

The most extreme description of the Island inhabitants in those days has been credited to a Major L. A. M. Jones in an article written in 1927 under the title "The Ten Thousand Islands." A part of this assessment is as follows:

> The islands, of which comparatively few are inhabited, are separated from each other by a system of tortuous and shallow channels, which are more confusing than any maze. Only an Islander can find his way through them, and as each man discreetly confines himself to the immediate neighborhood of his own particular island, there is probably not a single inhabitant to whom all the channels are known. The U. S. Government once put up signposts to mark a channel for yachts. The Islanders quickly rendered them useless by turning them in all directions but the right one.
>
> The arrival of another fugitive from justice in these mournful solitudes soon spreads around in some mysterious way; but many will be the moons that must wax and wane, and long and close indeed the scrutiny of the newcomer and his movements from afar off, before any sign is given that his fellow exiles are aware even of his existence. . . .
>
> They have seven unwritten laws, outside the observance of which are other laws; religious or moral systems are anathema to them. They are:
>
> Suspect every man.
> Ask no questions.

Settle your own quarrels.
Never steal from an Islander.
Stick by him, even if you do not know him.
Shoot quick, when your secret is in danger.
Cover your kill.

But Mama had not heard any of this, only the warning from the boat captain who was taking her to the tiny fishing village of Everglades. Her plans had been to take passage on a boat that would leave in the morning and arrive at Everglades in the afternoon, but unfortunately, the boat, or its operators, had problems and the voyage was delayed until late in the afternoon. This way the trip would take all night, especially with the wind that was blowing. But Mama was still game and obligated to the superintendent, and the journey commenced. It was a sailing boat with very crude and limited overnight accommodations.

After the storm passed the journey went much better and they arrived at Everglades about the time dawn came. The sea had quieted. A lady from the school people there met her and took her home, where she got some sleep, a bath, and a fine meal. About mid-afternoon of the same day, in a smaller sailboat with two men and a woman who was going to see a sick child, she completed her journey to Chokoloskee.

Conditions there were not as bad as at Alva. The school house was skimpy, but the parents of the children were more interested and cooperative.

Mama liked the people and they liked her. She thought many times that the man on the sailboat was just mischievously frightening her as he talked in such ominous and unrealistic terms of the slow living in the picturesque community surrounded by mangroves and water.

The four months commitment ended, and Mama made her way back to North Florida wiser, though not richer except in the experience of pioneering a new land with new people seeking knowledge from a few old books.

*   *   *   *   *

Since her days there Mama has been warmly interested in every drop of news involving Chokoloskee. One day a few years back she called to tell me that she had heard about a fierce outlaw named Edgar J. Watson who lived at Chatham Bend near Chokoloskee. The events, so grisly and unreal, actually transpired over a period ten to fifteen years after Mama left the area.

I learned the story from some clippings she had gathered and from what she had heard in conversations on a revisit to Chokoloskee, as well as from some additional research, and this is the way it went:

Edgar J. Watson was born near Lake City, Florida, in 1855. While still a young man, he left that area under hot pressure from a pursuing sheriff. Exactly what the trouble was is subject to considerable doubt, but most people heard "a nigger had been shot" and it was thought that Watson had done it. Watson went to Chatham Bend on the southwest coast of Florida on the edge of the Everglades to hide from the law. After a while, there was trouble at Chatham Bend and the sheriff came from Key West looking for Watson, who, his intelligence had indicated, was the prime suspect. But, again, Watson's special senses had warned him of danger and he had pulled out, this time for Texas or Arkansas.

There Watson entered some business relationships with Belle Starr, notorious woman outlaw of that time. The two were reported to have quarrelled, however, and a short time later Belle was murdered and Watson accused of the crime. But the authorities there couldn't catch him. He next showed up in Oregon where he was married and had several children. He got in trouble there too. Somebody shot a blast through the window of his house but he was not injured. He thought he knew who it was, found him the next morning, and shot him. Before he could be apprehended, he struck out for Florida, leaving his family behind.

Back at Chatham Bend, he became very successful in

producing sugar cane. He made syrup and cut timber both
of which he marketed in Key West. He ran boats, sometimes taking passengers between points on the lower West
Coast and in the Ten Thousand Islands. Success must have
bored him, and he got into a scrape with a man named
Bass who lived in Arcadia, and shot and killed him. His
extraordinary powers of rationalizing his crimes got him
free once more, but he was soon in trouble again. In another scrape, he cut a man's throat. The victim was
Adolphas Santini of Chokoloskee. He got clear of charges
for this, it was thought, by paying Mr. Santini a sum of
money to cover his damages. He brought his wife and
children from Oregon around this time but his wife died
a year later.

Watson bought a tract of land bordering on Lost Man's
River. A squatter moved on it and tenaciously refused
Watson's demands that he move. In a matter of days, the
squatter and his nephew were shot and killed, with Watson getting the full blame. This, again, was Watson's signal
to get going, and he went back to his birthplace in Colum-
bia County in North Florida, where he bought another
farm. A little later he had a dispute with two of his neighbors there and they were found murdered. He beat this
charge, too; but it wasn't easy. With smart lawyers who
managed to exact all the money and resources he had left
for fees, he was once more free, and penniless. Understandably, he returned to the pursuit in which he had been
most successful, syrup making at Chatham Bend. For help
in his fields, he is reported to have hired a white woman,
two white men, and a Negro man. When these people insisted upon pay for their labors, the hot tempered Watson
is said to have become furious. All of them were said to
have been murdered by a black employee of Watson's, and
the presumption was that the man who actually did the
killing was only carrying out Watson's orders.

His son, Robert, ran away to Key West, sold his father's
schooner there and returned to Oregon. Watson believed

that a man named Collins had given him wrong information about his son and, in an outrage of temper, attacked him.

By this time, the Islanders were alarmed to the point that they were deathly afraid of Watson. Watson apparently sensed that the people of the area were determined to lodge criminal charges against him and have him jailed, and as a defensive maneuver, he went to the sheriff at Ft. Myers and blamed the murder of his employees on a man named Cox. He demanded that the sheriff arrest Cox and charge him with the crimes. When the sheriff did not do as directed claiming bad weather as an excuse, Watson vowed that he would kill Cox himself. In a few days, the Islanders learned that Cox indeed had been murdered.

At this point the Islanders felt certain that they would have to take the law into their own hands.

The word was passed that Watson had gathered a motley group of outlaws at Chatham Bend preparing all kinds of outrageous, vengeful wrongs against those who might get in their way. Also it was learned that Watson would be coming to Chokoloskee on his boat one afternoon. The Islanders got ready for him. A small crowd had assembled at the landing, all fully armed. As he approached, Watson saw the reception committee waiting, and he must have known something of what he was in for. Nevertheless he walked and faced them. A quarrel quickly developed and Watson pointed a shotgun toward his accusers and snapped it twice but his shells were wet and wouldn't fire. Then he started for his six shooter, but by this time a volley of shots came from the group and he fell dead, thus ending the life of Florida's most notorious gunman.

The body was buried first on Rabbit Key, but later moved by members of his family to the cemetery in Ft. Myers. A stone marks the grave and upon it is the simple inscription, "Edgar J. Watson—November 11, 1855, October 24, 1910."

* * * * *

After learning of Mr. Watson's escapades ending at Mama's beloved Chokoloskee, I asked her, "Do you remember the name of the man with whom you talked on the boat who had such a harsh opinion of law and order in Chokoloskee?"

"I'm not sure about it," she replied.

"Was it—could it have been—Watson?" I asked.

It slowly dawned on her what I was suggesting. I could see that she was fixing dates and counting, and she said slowly, "Roy, you don't suppose—you don't really think it could have been the man on the boat do you?"

"Oh, not likely," I said. And she seemed quite relieved.

Richard Keith Call, Governor.

Courtesy of State of Florida

11

☆　☆　☆　☆　☆

The House of Call

ON JANUARY 10, 1861, as the crisp morning broke on the browning fields and pine-studded hills of his Lake Jackson Plantation, northwest of Tallahassee, General Richard Keith Call was about his usual chores. The bright, orange sun soon sparkled on the sprawling, grass-fringed lake dispersing the last misty remnants of nighttime and this seemed to be the cue for the wild things, each in its own special way, to greet the new day.

Astride his favorite riding horse, the General was checking on the day's work plans for the slaves who tilled his soil and saw to the comforts of his home. The General, now sixty-nine, was going to town early, and preparations of horse and buggy for the journey were going forward. His faithful slave, Abraham—the General insisted that the name not be shortened—would drive him. Since Call had taken up the life of plantation owner and operator, and had put down the burdens of public officeholding, so much of which he had carried from his boyhood, Abraham drove him on all his trips, taking care of his needs, including being a good listener to the often vehement expression of political views which seemed to be a permanent addiction of his master. Abraham could not understand what was said on some subjects, but he had developed a good set of approving nods and grunts, which greatly pleased and satisfied his master.

General Call was going to town to have his last say on

151

a subject which riled him deeply. Less than two months
before, Governor Madison S. Perry had recommended to
the Legislature that a convention be called to meet in Tallahassee on that January 3, 1861, to protect the rights of
the State of Florida, and the Legislature had so ordered.
The result was sure to be that Florida would join other
Southern states in seceding from the United States. Call
had been heavily involved in the debates, discussions, and
arguments on this subject that had gone before. He was
pro-slavery to the core. He held the paternalistic view of
the good, kind, slave master: The Negro was inherently
deficient, and limited in his ability to achieve. It would
take many generations of slavery under fair and beneficent
treatment before he could be logically granted equal rights
of citizenship. But, even so, Call could not bring himself
to approve any act in defiance of the United States. "I
should not despair of the glorious Union," he had written,
"It is . . . the government of a great people."

All his arguments had proved like the finger pressed
into the dam breach. There was no real chance for him to
stem the tide of such an avalanche of popular opinion.
Secession was sure to be voted that morning, pro forma.
And yet, the aging, frontier warrior still wanted to have
his say. His total life had been given to the advancement
of the welfare of Florida as a Territory and as a State, and
in her moments of suicide he wanted to shout, if nothing
more, "Don't! Do not forsake our union!"

As the horse and buggy jogged easily the eight miles to
Tallahassee, Call wondered if he would be heard by the
convention. There had been no invitation for him to express his views, but he felt that if he appeared, surely they
would not deny to him the floor.

His home on the edge of Tallahassee, The Grove, was
just over the next hill now as he neared the town limits.
He would drop in and see his daughter, Ellen, who was
living there with her two children. Her husband, Medicus
Long, had moved to Texas. Ellen and her father had al-

ways enjoyed a very close relationship. She was ten years older than her only sister, Mary. When the girls' mother had died Mary was an infant. Ellen was attending school in Maryland. In answer to her father's letter telling her of their great loss, the ten-year-old wrote to her father:

> "I will do anything to make you happy. I shall hereafter try to obey you in everything. I feel very sorry that I ever displeased you or mother."

She had kept her pledge faithfully and with great devotion. Her sister, the second Mary Call, also lived in Tallahassee. She was married to a prominent local lawyer and budding political leader, Theodore W. Brevard. The Brevard family lived in a house nearby which Mary and her husband had acquired independently.

They could have taken a short-cut going into the back of The Grove property, but Abraham and the General both liked to go in proudly at the front. As they turned into the grounds around ten o'clock that morning, the moss-draped live oak trees framed the magnificent columns supporting the high pediment of the classic Greek revival structure. The General never failed to be stirred when he looked upon this house and warmed by the memories it kindled.

Ellen ran down the front steps to greet her father and arm in arm they walked up the broad steps to the open porch and on into the wide, high-ceilinged, central hall. With coat and hat put up, the two moved into the large living room and sitting by the crackling fire Ellen talked gayly of the house, her children, and her plans for them. The house had three floors, each with the same wide hall extending from front to back and two large rooms on each side opening into it. Each room had a fireplace and the large doors and windows were framed with moldings reflecting simple dignity. The circular stairway from the main floor hall to the top floor was almost a duplicate of the one at the Hermitage, Andrew Jackson's house near Nashville.

Family cemetery back of The Grove.

When Call told his daughter of his intentions to go down to the capitol and address the convention, she was frank in her disapproval. She explained the futility of it, and finally talked the General into having the noonday meal with her and leaving the convention to its own designs.

While they were eating later, a messenger from the capitol came to inquire if Call was there. The General thought at first that he was to be invited to address the convention after all. But no such invitation was delivered; and the messenger soon left, making it clear that it was only Call's presence in town that he was directed to confirm. An hour later another messenger came with the word that the convention had adjourned and some of the delegates were on their way out to see Call.

They came in high spirits, and standing at the foot of

the front steps they called for Call to come out on the porch. They wanted to confront their victim in their hour of triumph and taunt him in his hour of defeat. Call promptly accommodated them. He came out erect and proud, waving his cane high above his head, as if it held a banner, or perhaps to show that he was not dependent upon it for support.

"Well, Governor," his visitors shouted, "We have done it."

"And what have you done?" replied the General in true Socratic style. Then after a pause during which he stared at first one and then another, he answered his own question in carefully measured cadence: "You have opened the gates of hell, from which shall flow the curses of the damned which shall sink you to perdition." With that he lowered his cane, turned about, and with head still high, walked stiffly back into the house.

Ellen met him as he came through the door, put her arms around him, saying softly, "You just can't stop fighting, can you? Don't you remember General Jackson once told you, 'Don't break your shins on stools when you can honorably remove them'."

To this the General replied, "Why that's what I was doing, Ellen, honorably pushing them away. It was all I could do to keep from going down those steps and breaking my stick on the first skull I could reach."

An hour or so later Call said that he wanted to walk around the grounds. Alone, he first found a japonica tree that had a few brave early deep red blossoms. Picking one he wandered down through the oaks, magnolia and walnut trees, behind the big house to the little family cemetery close by. This was a favorite habit of his and Ellen knew he wished to be alone. A large tree had fallen in the plot set aside for the graves, but miraculously it had not disturbed any grave or stone or vault. Call had asked that its limbs be trimmed off but that the trunk not be removed. He liked to sit there and let his mind run at random. He placed the japonica on the vault where Mary Kirkman Call was buried, then sat down. The top slab of Mary's vault had this inscription:

Mary K. Call
wife of
General Richard K. Call
Died in the 33rd year
of her age, the 28th
day of February, 1836
"Distinguished for every virtue
exemplary in every condition of
life. She lived beloved and
died lamented by all who knew her"

Memories of Mary came rushing in. Joyous times from their early acquaintance in Nashville—his unsuccessful efforts to obtain the approval of her strong-willed and wealthy mother for their marriage. It was not so much the young man, Richard Call, she didn't like, but he was an Indian fighter of Andrew Jackson's and the Kirkmans weren't fond of Jackson, his frontier manners or military ventures. Besides, Call wanted to make his home in the "wild" Territory of Florida and Mrs. Kirkman did not want her daughter subjected to the hazards of such a life.

Now Call looked about him in the cemetery and said to himself, "God, as it turned out she was so right." Mary, during their life together (twelve years), had given birth to eight children there at The Grove. The first, Ellen, was born in 1825, before the big house was finished and they were occupying a temporary cottage. Six were buried there, the oldest having lived only three years; two were buried in one casket, Richard Jackson Call, one year old, and Mary Ann Call, three years old. Two more babies, twins, did not live long enough to be given names.

Oh, the dreadful day when Mary died. The General didn't want to think of this, but he couldn't keep it out of his mind. Mary had been seriously ill and he was worried deeply about her in those latter days of February 1836. But she and the doctor thought she was much better and that he should take his company of militia on down to Tampa, as directed by the President, to help subdue the Indians. She seemed so much better when he left for St. Marks, where he and his men were to embark on the Revenue Cutter *Dallas*.

On February 28, Call and his troops had boarded the ship and had moved down the river when a black servant of Call's rode into St. Marks. Finding his master gone, he dashed to a point of land farther out, got a small boat, and managed to get close enough to the cutter to attract Call's attention. The ship was stopped, and Call learned from the servant that Mary's condition had seriously worsened and that he should return home immediately. He sent his men on and started for Tallahassee on a horse he rode so hard that it dropped dead as it reached the driveway of The Grove. There he learned that his beloved Mary had died, and he had felt that his life also was gone.

They buried her that night by torchlight. He could remember the service so well. The casket was brought from the back of the house by Tallahassee friends. Slaves broken with sorrow stood on each side holding torches marking the way for the procession. Others held flowers. Many friends from the community gathered. Some of the blacks were singing spirituals as the whole group moved down under the oak trees and gathered right at the very place he now sat. The minister from St. John's Episcopal Church, which he had helped found and served as member of its first vestry, had read the sad words and prayers which told of hope and eternal rewards.

But then the General turned gently that sad page in his book of life, and came to others which told of joys that he and Mary had known together.

Their marriage on July 15, 1824. When he went by her home in Nashville to take her to the nearby Hermitage of Andrew Jackson for the ceremony, he didn't see the disapproving mother-in-law to be, Mrs. Kirkman, but

there must have been a hundred people there to wish
them well. General and Mrs. Jackson had been such wonderful friends, taking them into their own beautiful home
for this great moment of their lives. It was a home Call
had known well from countless prior visits and that both
came to know almost as well as their own in the years
ahead. Call was then thirty-two, Mary twenty-three. He
was well established in the Florida territory with his home
base in Pensacola.

After his Indian campaigns with Jackson, he had, with
little preparation, commenced the practice of law there.
He was appointed by President Monroe to the territorial
Legislative Council, where his leadership abilities became
quickly evident. This was a springboard to his election
as the territorial delegate to the United States Congress.
His first session in Washington in 1823 was one of conspicuous success for him. He roomed there with then U. S.
Senator Andrew Jackson, who had served as Florida's first
territorial governor. The two were very close friends and
strong political allies. Four days after Call was sworn in
as territorial delegate in Washington, he successfully
sponsored action to commit the Congress to the location
and establishment of a Florida territorial capital and to
providing a grant of land for this purpose.

He also handled successfully other measures for the
development of the territory, including the construction
of roads and bridges. Senator Jackson gave a steadfast
and helping support all the way, and his feelings of friendship were ardently reciprocated.

It was after this session that the marriage took place,
and Call, after a two-months stay in Tennessee, returned
to Florida alone to make preparations about his future
residence and to prepare for the forthcoming new session
of the Congress. When the Tallahassee capital site was
selected in 1824 by Commissioners Williams and Simmons,
he was very pleased and immediately began making his
plans to establish his home there.

He took Mary with him to resume his duties in Washington and they both enjoyed life there. At the close of the next session of Congress, he brought Mary to Pensacola where she was very happy. Enroute, they stopped in New Orleans and visited the Marquis de Lafayette, whom they had come to know well in Washington.

The new community of Tallahassee, Call always felt, was a part of his own creation. He had sponsored the congressional action under which it had been established, and now he had moved there in 1824 to make his permanent residence. He bought lands within less than a mile from the first log structure that served to house the governmental headquarters. On these lands, he and Mary dreamed of building a house of great beauty. Call was determined that it be even more beautiful than the Nashville home in which Mary's family had lived.

Before the year 1824 was out, they had built a temporary house to live in until their big house could be built. It was on the grounds and very near the site of the later big house. Ellen was born there, "the first white child" to be born in the area after the capital was established there. The Grove, the name Mary gave the big house because of the beautiful stand of live oaks that adorned the site, was to grow in stages over the years ahead. Call's income had to grow to pay for it, the lumber had to be cut and dried on the place, the brick had to be made— also on the place. From its beginning in 1825, historians have reckoned that it must have taken at least six years before it was ready to be occupied. As it took form, it gave charm and distinction to its proud owners, reflecting their tastes and cultural aspirations. In turn, Mary and her husband gave it the full measure of their interest, love, and care.

Oh, the excitement of the years that followed: Jackson was inaugurated president in 1829, and Tallahassee by that time had grown to a population of 1,000, with three hotels, two private schools, eleven stores, and one grogshop.

Miniature of Lt. Richard Keith Call just before his marriage and move to Tallahassee.

General Call, accompanied by Mrs. Call and Ellen, visited Jackson in the White House. Call remained one of Jackson's closest friends, notwithstanding Call's distrust of Peggy Eaton, and the irritation resulting from Jackson's determined support of her moral character.

Call became a very successful lawyer, handling many important cases in the courts of North Florida and South Georgia. He handled cases also before the United States Supreme Court in Washington.

The Seminoles were becoming more and more belligerent and Call felt impelled from his military experience in fighting Indians earlier to become more deeply involved. He wanted badly to command the Florida militia, and he wanted to resume his public service career.

The General's recollections now came back to the

Miniature of Mary (Kirkman) Call just before her marriage—gift to her husband.

Courtesy of Mrs. George H. Gwynn

times of agony—for the efforts he had made in operations against the Indians had brought to him severe and unjust criticism.

He was saddened, too, in recalling that Mary could not share with him the pride and satisfaction of the years he served as governor of the territory of Florida. It was not until a few weeks after her death that President Jackson appointed him to serve his first term as governor.

He was aware now that he was not alone on the log— a cheerful male voice said, "Uncle Richard, cousin Ellen said you were down here and that I could come. She will have some hot tea ready soon and then if you and Abraham are going to make it back to the lake before dark you will need to get underway." This was George Call, Jr., son of his brother, George, who had followed him to Florida. The nephew was a fine, clean-cut, young man in his twenties and a strong favorite of the General's.

As the two walked toward the house, George, who had heard of the secession action earlier and of the confrontation at The Grove steps, asked his uncle, "How do you really see this thing coming out?"

"Well, it just means war," the General said. "The United States cannot let the states decide each for itself whether to be in or out. The Union was put together under a constitution which binds all for the common good. I don't care for Lincoln. I think black people are better off as well-provided-for slaves than they could be as freed men. But the Union question is bigger than Lincoln, bigger than slaves. It's a question of our life as a nation."

"Can the South win if war comes?" George asked.

The General shook his head. "Not a chance, as I see it," he said. "We haven't got what it takes. Now, we can drag it out and win some engagements sure, but it's the long pull that will tell. We can't stand it: the United States can. It's like starting off a checker game with one-half the men your opponent has. He can kill you even if he has to give you two for every one he takes."

After tea, the General persuaded young Richard Call Long, Ellen's fifteen year old son, to return with him to the plantation on the lake.

The General enjoyed having Richard with him on the plantation. Often they rode, hiked, hunted and fished over the plantation lands and waters together. The General had tried to teach this youth much of what he had learned from life, starting with his advanced agricultural experimentation; the construction of the railroad to St. Marks, one of the country's first; his efforts to establish a new city near St. Marks, Port Leon; his service as territorial governor over two separate periods; his party feuds and fights in the state; his controversies with Washington over the Indian wars; the ins and outs, the ups and downs, of his tumultous political career; and most of all, his faith in the principles of Andrew Jackson and his deep pride in the relationship he had had with him since he organized his little company of school boys at Mount Pleasant Academy in Tennessee and took them to join Jackson in fighting Indians when he was only twenty years of age.

The General had told Richard not to get into politics unless he became sure of a few things about himself— could he stand the gaff of untrue criticism calculated to bring dishonor upon him and destroy his public support? Next, could he hold steadfast to the course he thought to be best for all the people under pressure to do otherwise, not only from enemies but often from good friends? Could he keep the agony of defeat from destroying him? A man just has to lose on some issues, he explained. He is almost sure to be wrong and deserves to lose at times and at other times he will be right but the public will not understand this. When he loses he ought to take it, bide his time, then come back. This is hard to do, but you've got to get it in your soul and let it come out in your actions that no one, can take away your honor and dignity as a responsible man. This way you can take a lot of abuse and keep the kind of clear head that will allow you to win a lot of tough fights.

All this was the voice of his own experience.

He talked of the pride he had in his country, in his state, in his community. This, he explained, he could feel mainly because for all these he had given so much of his own energies and efforts. Every time he went to the capitol building, he explained, he felt pride because of what he had done to make the territorial government strong and effective; for his efforts during both his terms as governor to build upon true principles; for his efforts to develop the first constitution under which the territory could be accepted as a state; for his efforts to build the state government subsequently. The capitol building it-

self was built while he was territorial governor, with
moneys obtained through his own efforts and from authority granted by the Federal government. The contract
had been let and the work supervised by him.

All these things Call emphasized in his talks with his
grandson because he felt they would challenge and in-
spire the boy as he grew toward manhood.

The two persons he talked most with, however, were
his daughters, Ellen and Mary. Every detail of the planning of The Grove he later shared with them because
as he put it, "Someday you will own it. It will demand
much from you just as it will give much to you."

He explained many details of its construction. "The
house was built on the frontier, remember that. Our object
was to create a house that would combine strength and
utility with beauty. It is not ornate. Its lines are simple and
reflect a purity of design. We tried to build it strong enough
to live forever and give to it a style that would best fit this
climate and that would be beautiful forever.

"There is no steel above any of the windows or door
openings. Nor are there any wooden structural supports
for these openings. The bricks were laid utilizing the arch
principle and this makes the openings secure. We used
many people in the work. Some, of course, were trained
and brought in, but the help of our untrained Negroes
also was essential. The outside walls and the interior
divisions between the rooms are all solid brick: 17 inches
thick at the ground, 14 inches thick at the second story
level, and 11 inches thick at the upper room level. Every
wall is continuous from the ground to the top. This will
enable the house to withstand well any storm and the
deterioration of age.

"The house was never finished. An iron balcony was
planned across the front portico under the upper windows.
The brackets were provided and still protrude, but the
balcony never arrived from England where it was custom-

made. The ship on which it was sent was wrecked trying to navigate the Florida Straits and it was never salvaged. News of this came just after Mary's death and for some time we all just lost heart. This was her house, you know. The little ornamental caps for the fluted columns by the side of the front entrance also never came. Chocks of wood were wedged in pending their arrival, and still remain in place. [They are still there to this day.] The front columns are made of brick, wedge-shaped, with a cement outer coating. The lime and cement were shipped by water to St. Marks.

"You and Mary must love this house for us, as well as for yourselves and for all those who will come later. Keep it in the family as long as there are those in the family who care and are able to maintain it. Never let it be dishonored or abused and it will love and honor you and those to come later."

With Florida's secession and his deeper concern about the ravages of the ever-recurring fever that had eroded his health, Call withdrew more and more from outside contacts. He was content now with the love of his family, the protective embrace of The Grove, and the continuing challenge of his fields at Lake Jackson.

Politically, along with Sam Houston of Texas and other leaders who grew up under the personal guidance and with the deep affection of Andrew Jackson, he would be a Unionist always. He could never tolerate a concept of separated states which he saw as becoming ultimate pawns for other strong nations to push about. It was in the strong union of states that he saw the whole hopes of the nation, and of the world.

Yet, like other Southern leaders, a conflict now arose between national loyalty and the loyalty of man with man, man with family, man with community, man with state. Having given so much to, and received so much from, his community and his state, Call could not turn his back on these, whatever his regret over, and disapproval of, the events that led to the present situation of State vs. Union. So, as the occasions arose, Call professed his loyalty to and support of the South. But more than ever before in his adult lifetime he kept his counsel, and those who saw him knew that the brooding and doubt deepened, though the news of Southern successes in the early months of 1862 was rather optimistic.

Then two things happened in the spring and summer of that year: there was a break of the Confederate strength in Mississippi and, as Call confided in a written message to Ellen: "It indicates the abandonment of the West, and the approach of the death struggle at Richmond. It will be terrible and fatal. The short and brilliant military career of the Southern Confederacy will end like the going down of the sun. . . ."

Then the news came that George Call, Jr., who had enlisted in the Confederate cause soon after the secession, had been killed in battle. This information seemed to pull a last prop out from under the General, and he asked Abraham to take him back to The Grove. There, Ellen and Mary attended him constantly and saw that he had all the medical help possible to relieve his pain. But the General felt that he had finished his fight.

September 14, 1862, was a Sunday. Tallahassee was close to the path of a hurricane and the rain was coming down with high winds driving fusillades of stinging wet pellets against the large windows of the General's bedroom. The oaks outside strained to hold onto their limbs that were twisting and bending in grotesque shapes. Ellen and Mary thought the storm might disturb the General, but, to the contrary, he was comforted by its fury and asked to be left alone. They went out around four o'clock in the afternoon and, returning after a few minutes, they found that their father had finished the course of his life.

In the early morning hours of the 16th, they buried

him as he wished—in the little Grove cemetery by the
side of Mary, his wife, and close by the graves of their six
babies, dead at the age of three and under.

Mary and the six children were victims of the frontier.
Only the General had been its master, and he only for
a time. This house would stand as the most enduring
witness.

ELLEN CALL LONG
(Defender of the Faith)

Ellen Call Long grew in the image of her father. She
was physically strong, as he was. She had extraordinary
intellectual capacity, as he had. They shared a common
dynamism of thought, word, and action. As Margaret
Chapman, distinguished Florida historian and archivist
said in her introduction to the facsimile reproduction of
Mrs. Long's *Florida Breezes* in 1962, "they shared the
same generous and affectionate nature and the same deadly
sin of pride, to the point of arrogance."

The passion of Ellen's life was to extol and vindicate
her father's actions and opinions, and she brought her
considerable talents as a writer and communicator to the
task of accomplishing this. She was well educated. Much
of her youth had been spent attending schools in the
North and this experience insulated her against the highly
emotional provincialism so dominant in the South of her
days. Thus, she sought to rationalize her positions on
stronger supports than regional pride alone.

She always felt that her father was abused, mostly because of his strong belief in, and willingness to stand up
and fight for, the Union. Her conviction was in line with
that of her contemporary, Emerson, that "to be great is
to be misunderstood," and it was her mission to minimize
the misunderstanding. After the General's death and after
the war had ended, she extended herself to help reestablish

Ellen (Call) Long at The Grove.

a sense of national loyalty in the South because she felt he would have done this. She became actively involved in the plans for the Centennial Exposition to be held in Philadelphia in 1876, serving as a leader in the State of Florida's efforts. This involved various fund raising events from the panhandle to Key West. In most of these the going was exceedingly difficult. Few Floridians were ready then to cooperate in "Yankee" projects. She took an active part in raising contributions to help in the purchase of Mount Vernon and the establishment there of a National Washington Shrine. When Mrs. Yulee, Florida regent of the Mount Vernon Association, failed to attend meetings, it was suggested by those in high authority that she resign and that Mrs. Long be named to succeed her, but this idea was rejected by Mrs. Long, perhaps out of respect for Mrs. Yulee.

She traveled widely over the nation under appointments to various commissions by Florida governors and went as a delegate from Florida to the Paris Exposition in 1889 by appointment of Governor Edward A. Perry.

In the meantime, her personal finances were coming under heavy strain, and her immediate family circumstances deteriorated.

Mrs. Long had two children, a son, Richard, and a daughter, Eleanora (Mrs. E. K. Hollinger). Richard had two children, a daughter, Reinette Gamble Long and a son also named Richard Call Long. Ellen found herself burdened to keep up the Grove and to support and care for Richard and his family who stayed with her for many years.

Mrs. Hollinger was there too some of the years and sought to supplement the income of the group by giving piano lessons. One of her students was Mr. A. Bernard Byrd who remembers well his experiences at The Grove sitting with Mrs. Hollinger on the bench of the huge grand piano.

"She was a wonderful teacher—a happy young lady

Eleanora Kirkman (Long) Hollinger, "The Tallahassee Girl," in 1875.
Courtesy of R. R. Hollinger

whose eyes sparkled as she talked with you," he recalled. "I remember that on occasions when we were working Mrs. Long [Ellen] would suddenly appear. Everything immediately stopped, and you got the feeling that the king had entered and the only appropriate move would be to rise and bow low. She was a commanding, imperious person in her physical presence. She was large but she carried her weight like she was supposed to have every bit of it. Her voice was husky, and strong. Before she spoke, Mrs. Hollinger would acknowledge her presence by simply saying 'Yes, ma-ma.' Mrs. Long would then say 'Nonie' (that's what most of the older people called Mrs.

Hollinger). Then, because I assume she did not want me to know what the conversation was about Mrs. Long would start speaking French and the two would finish their conversation back and forth in that language and it was all done with a real flair."

Mr. Byrd also mentioned that not all of his music lessons were at The Grove. "I could be downtown, anywhere almost, and if I happened to run into Mrs. Hollinger she would say, 'Come, Bernard, let me give you a lesson.' Then she would lead me into the nearest house that had a piano and proceed to teach me by the grace of whoever happened to own it. She was so popular that people seemed to be honored by these interruptions."

One of Mrs. Long's friends and visitors was the distinguished novelist of his time, Maurice Thompson* who in 1881 published *A Tallahassee Girl*. The book was acclaimed with pride in Florida and widely sold throughout the country. It was generally recognized from the descriptions that the principal character was inspired by Mrs. Long's beautiful daughter "Nonie," and that the fictional home of the heroine clearly was The Grove. In fact, for many years afterward The Grove almost lost its name in the public mind as it became commonly referred to as the "Home of the Tallahassee Girl."

Mrs. Long sought to shore up her diminishing resources through writing and publishing. *The Battle of New Orleans: Jackson and Pakenham,* a pamphlet, was published in New Orleans, in 1885. Her chief work has been said to be *Florida Breezes* which was published in Jacksonville, the first printing in 1882. It is a fictional launching of much sturdy fact regarding antebellum times in the Tallahassee area, including social life as well as the political turmoil of the period between 1820 and 1845. There is much that she took from conversations and the writings

---

*Mr. Thompson was the grandfather of Mr. Lee Ballard, former chairman of the Florida Board of Control, and present banker and businessman of Pinellas County.

of her father, and convincing vindication of his leadership, competence, and integrity.

Once Mrs. Long turned to what she felt would be a money-making scheme of raising silk worms and producing silk at The Grove. She did an exhaustive job of researching her project in cooperation with other interested ladies of the capital city. The highly innovative experiment was undertaken in one of the small cottages at the rear of The Grove. There remains considerable doubt about who enjoyed the operation most, the ladies or the worms. It was one of those successful operations though the patient died. The worms, under much stimulation, produced silk all right—enough for the ladies to make a gorgeous American flag pretentious in size and color which was duly and with ceremony presented to the State on the occasion of the inauguration of Governor Edward A. Perry.* Further, as a result of these experiments Mrs. Long published in Philadelphia an illustrated monograph *Silk Farming in Florida* which was widely distributed.

There were other manuscripts she wrote dealing with Florida history, including the completion of the Call Journal after the death of her father. The General had written much of his life story but was unable to finish it prior to his final illness.

Margaret Chapman, in her *Florida Breezes* reprint introduction, describes Ellen Call Long in these terms: "[She] would have been a remarkable woman in any age. In her own era she was truly exceptional. Though she

*Note: The Florida Times Union for January 7, 1885, carried the following in its report covering the inaugural:

THE PROCESSION

At half-past eleven the music of the band announced the approach of the procession of young ladies, who were to conduct the ceremony of presentation of the beautiful flag of Florida-grown silk to the State, attended by an escort composed of a battalion of the cadets of the West Florida Seminary under the command of Colonel E.R. Rivers, and a detatchment of the Governor's Guards forming a gun squad with a 12-pounder, commanded by Captain Alex Moseley.

The gaily uniformed little company, attended by a large number of pupils

Color guard of Tallahasseeans that presented the flag made of silk produced at The Grove at Governor Perry's inauguration.

cherished what was best in plantation life in the old South, she did not turn inward to a tight, provincial society as did many Southerners. She remained cosmopolitan rather than provincial in outlook. She lived by certain steadfast rules. 'I have always been a truthful and honorable woman in all business matters . . . and in all matters of care taking. I have been natural and generous to those depending on me.' She reacted to all situations as her conscience guided her, and was not swayed by public opinion."

of the seminary, took up their positions immediately in front of the portico, the artillery on the left and the cadets on the right, and in the rear a color guard of cadets, having been detailed for the purpose under the command of Cadet Captain Shine, occupied a central position supporting color-bearer Cadet Carter who bore the presentation flag. At the rear, Sergeant Ellis, an ex-Federal soldier and for many years a trusted attache at the Capitol, bore aloft the beautiful State banner of Florida.

Miss Chapman then documents this assessment by relating a truly remarkable happening for those times. Former Governor Harrison Reed, aware of her economic pressures, had written Mrs. Long suggesting that she seek the appointment of postmaster for Tallahassee. She responded by saying the job was "not to my taste" and also disclosing that she had committed her support to a Negro applicant, a Reverend William A. Stewart. Then she added, "It is a conviction of mine that when a Negro proves himself worthy morally and capable intellectually of the rewards of citizenship by the practice of honesty, and soberness and discretion, he is entitled to enter the list for competitive places of preferment. This doctrine was taught by Republican pioneers in Florida and if in its adoption, I out-Herod, Herod, by a practical recognition of said tenets, it must be charged to that earnestness with which I always believe or disbelieve."

This was unpopular philosophy in Florida for her time, but with her father's precepts Ellen's voice and actions rang true.

Maintaining The Grove, which her father had deeded to her before his death, and continuing the style of life to which she was accustomed, became an ever more difficult task for her.

She was forced to part with many treasures that over the years had become intimate parts of The Grove itself. Mr. Henry Flagler, who built the railroad down the East Coast of Florida and on to Key West, visited her on several occasions and obtained some items including the purchase of two large cement corner stones which General Call had acquired when Fort San Marcos at St. Marks, built by the Spaniards, was finally abandoned. According to Mrs. Long:

> This is a structure built of the limestone of the country, quarried in the neighborhood by the captive Creeks and Seminoles, on which work they must have been employed many years. There are two stones that tell its ori-

Ellen (Call) Long in 1895.

gin. One bears the coat of arms of Spain, Castile and Leon—Thunderbolts, Golden Fleece and Crown; the other proclaims that the fort was built in the time of his Catholic Majesty, Ferdinand VI, of Spain, A. D. 1753. It has bomb-proof walls, with bastions mounting a flat room, and at intervals embrasures for guns and there is a parapet finish.

The General had kept one of the stones on each side of the entrance gates of The Grove. Mrs. Long made a gift to Mr. Flagier of two items that had been given to Call by Andrew Jackson: an original oil portrait of Jackson and a field desk which Jackson had used in his military campaigns. She said that Mr. Flagler had offered and paid so much for the stones that she felt she should not charge for the other items.

The house also had in its early days beautiful marble mantles which are no longer there, and which it is presumed were also stripped off sorrowfully and sold by Mrs. Long.

As she grew older, her principal income came from the sale of lots carved from the original Grove place. Bit by agonizing bit she was forced to consume those things which were precious parts of her own life.

Her son, Richard, was of little or no productive help and became an invalid in her care. Soon after the turn of the century she had a $3,000 mortgage on The Grove she could not discharge and foreclosure and loss of the property were imminent. Her granddaughter, Reinette, had married a Mr. E. C. Hunt and moved to New York. They came back, however, and Mr. Hunt, who was presumed to be a man of substantial means, offered to help. Mrs. Long understood that he would go to New York and solicit a new loan to refinance the debt, and as he requested, she signed papers which she understood would facilitate this. It later turned out that she had deeded The Grove property to Mr. Hunt, the conveyance being supported by the alleged consideration of his efforts and outlays in discharging the threatening mortgage debt.

This caused much family unhappiness and Mrs. Long accused her son, Richard, of being implicated with his daughter and her husband in a plot to take the property from her. He denied this and insisted that Mr. Hunt's efforts were of advantage to his mother resulting not only in saving The Grove but making it possible that she could live there for the rest of her life, with Mr. Hunt further providing an annuity for her support. (There is no record that any annuity was paid.)

This was Ellen Call Long's greatest agony since the loss

of her father. This house, her beautiful house, her blessed sanctuary, had slipped beyond her control. She felt a heavy burden of defeat and failure. Her proud and generous nature, accustomed to bestowing upon others, was, as she now felt, reduced to a status of dependence upon the charity of others. This she could not live with and took to her bed with a lingering illness.

A year later in the same massive room of The Grove in which her father died, she also breathed her last. She had kept the faith, though her last days were haunted by what would and could happen to The Grove in the future. She was buried in the cemetery behind the house in the trees, appropriately by the side of her father.

REINETTE LONG HUNT
(Entrepreneuse Extraordinaire)

Ellen Call Long made a handwritten will in the year before her death (1904). There was little to dispose of. Some of her interests in the plantation lands of her father had been acquired with her sister, Mary, and these would only last for their lives. The Grove property in Tallahassee and other Lake Jackson lands in which she had owned fee title had been deeded to Mr. Hunt in December 1903 and he, in turn, had conveyed them to his wife, Reinette Long Hunt (Ellen's granddaughter), the following March 4. Mrs. Long left what she had, mainly household furnishings and personal effects to her daughter, Mrs. Hollinger, thus by-passing her son, Richard, and his family. As she explained, she had done so much for Richard in his lifetime that she felt this was only fair. Doubtless, she also took into account that Reinette was Richard's daughter and would have The Grove and other lands by virtue of the prior deed.

Ellen's sister, Mary, was separated from her by a ten-year difference in their ages and later by other circumstances. Mary loved and greatly admired Ellen, but the

Reinette Gamble (Long) Hunt and Diogenes.

two had very different personalities, preferences, and interests; Ellen was like her father, Mary like her mother. Mary was quiet, not tempestuous. She was demure, not flamboyant. She loved her home and was wholly content with her family, feeling none of Ellen's call to operate in the public spotlight. Her business judgments were conservative, not erratic.

Mary had made a very successful home. Her husband was Theodore W. Brevard, a prominent lawyer and state senator of Tallahassee.

Mary had been born at The Grove, as had some of her children, including Jane Kirkman. It was for her family a place to go back to, but she respected her father's reasons for deeding it to Ellen. She had been saddened by Ellen's difficulties and had helped her in many ways. She was unhappy with the Hunts's intrusion and their gain of the title to The Grove and sympathized deeply with her niece, Mrs. Hollinger's, position. But she kept her feelings about this to herself.

Reinette Long Hunt's tenure at The Grove began in 1904 and ended with her death in 1940. This span of time was characterized by turbulence and traumatic developments which left deep scars on Reinette herself and deeper ones on The Grove.

The marriage of Reinette to Mr. Charles Edwin Hunt occurred in Tallahassee in 1897. She was then twenty-four and earlier had attended schools in the North though much of her childhood was spent at The Grove. She was aggressive by nature, liberal in her instincts, and expensive in her tastes. After her marriage, she and Mr. Hunt lived in New York; but apparently the lure of Tallahassee and The Grove continued to haunt her. Her mother, who lived elsewhere in Tallahassee, was a Gamble before her marriage. This was another prominent and highly respected family.

Reinette returned to Tallahassee often, considering transportation limitations of those days. Sometimes her

husband came with her; sometimes not. These Tallahassee visits and the consequent interruptions in their marriage relationship led to more and more incompatibility,
or vice versa, and in 1910 Reinette brought suit for divorce
in Tallahassee. The Circuit Court held against her, but
the Florida Supreme Court reversed the decision and set
Reinette free. The Court held that alleged grounds of de-
sertion and violent and ungovernable temper against Mr.
Hunt were adequately proved. There is no indication
that she ever heard from Hunt again, and it would appear
that he was as glad to be rid of her, as she of him.
There was no property settlement or alimony involved.

So Reinette, then thirty-eight, was left without husband,
without children, without support, except for The Grove
(which then included a plot 400 feet by 840 feet) and the
part interest in the Lake Jackson lands which had come
to her through General Call, her grandmother Ellen, and
the deed from her husband five or six years previously.

Reinette, however, was firmly established in The Grove
and had been since before her grandmother's death, and
this afforded her a strong base. Here, she maintained a
mighty struggle for her own individuality and for the survival of The Grove, and there were many times the two
objectives seemed impossible to reconcile.

Reinette was well educated in the liberal arts. She had
a pet dog that she carried around somewhat in the fashion
of Charles I. She named the dog "Diogenes," doubtless because of her great admiration for the eccentric Greek phi-
losopher who stressed belief in the simple life by living in
a tub and going about in the daylight carrying a lantern
looking for an honest man.

She found the furnishings in The Grove, after Mrs. Hollinger removed what Ellen had left to her, very meager
and she sought to augment them, but her tastes did not
run entirely with the first Mary Call's and Ellen's eighteenth century preferences, and the house became di-
sheveled.

Reinette painted pictures, both in oils and water colors. The process of developing a studio environment in The Grove did not cause her serious concern, but surely it must have caused the house some. She gave lessons in painting. She also taught dancing for a while, perhaps until her large size simply would not allow her to set any kind of reasonable example of form for her pupils to emulate. She could write well, and published a number of pamphlets, including the *Historical Pageant of Tallahassee, Osola, Welaunee,* and other Florida sketches. Hand painting on china and writing poetry were probably the two art forms she loved most and did best. She found a limited market for her literary and art works, and some income was realized from them. She loved the little town of Panacea on the Gulf Coast, southwest of Tallahassee, and spent most of her summers in a cottage she owned there.

Reinette was brusque with people she did not know, but this carried no intended abuse. She was warmly affectionate with her friends and often they gathered before her as if she were a swami and they the loyal and beholden. The Grove itself became, of course, an important part of her magnetism. It gave an aura of character and respectability to her views and mannerisms, no matter how they failed to conform with accepted traditions.

The hard times of the depression of the early thirties hit Reinette with great severity. She had no dependable income, no way to provide the bare essentials of life, no way to keep The Grove adequately maintained against the demands of the tax assessor and the normal attrition and erosion of time.

She had important help from two "inside" friends. David Floyd, her Negro house servant, cooked, served, and milked the cow. Further, he attended to many other menial tasks essential for the care of the house. He stayed with her not because of pay but because he had come under her own special magnetism and could not bring himself to leave. David knew Reinette well. When she invited guests for dinner, Reinette took her place at the head of the table which was beautifully arranged with service plates and soft candlelight. David, in frayed white coat, would serve with impeccable savoir faire. The food was expertly prepared. A dish that might elsewhere have been commonplace was, at Reinette's table, superb, the conversation and guests stimulating and sophisticated.

Robert Aldridge was another of Reinette's faithful friends. He lived in the basement of the house, or at times in one of the cottages behind, and was devoted to her. He was a man of extraordinary talents, distinctive background, and altogether a perfect example of the type who would find Reinette irresistible. Mr. Aldridge was trained as an engineer at Cornell. He came to Florida with a wife with whom he seemed always at war and who soon left him. He was very intelligent, read the best of literature, and kept up with current events around the world. One could not have found a better conversationalist. He was a handy man for Reinette to have around the house, installing a washer to stop a leaking faucet, or helping entertain guests for dinner, with equal competence.

Aldridge did not like the mundane business of work unless he was doing something for someone who cared. He wanted only to make enough money to keep himself going from one day to the next. He resented the "establishment" of his time and had such a concern for the underdog that he developed a reputation around legal circles as an excellent juror for a defendant charged with crime.

So Reinette, David Floyd, and Robert Aldridge went through the turbulent thirties as a team at The Grove, with Reinette supplying the vision and setting the course and the other two loyally and completely backing her up through all the trials and tribulations that ensued.

Like Ellen Call Long before her, Reinette was forced to turn to The Grove itself for something more than shelter, comfort, and distinction. She was forced by circumstances to exploit it.

She had tried without success, many local business ventures including one under the name of "Leon Storage and Seed Company." Then she sought the development of a public tearoom in the basement of The Grove. When this enterprise too proved unsuccessful, she turned to rentals, dividing parts of the house into apartments. She built a bathroom outside one of the large windows of the formal living room and divided this room into several smaller ones with beaver board partitions. The Grove dining room, which opened with large silver handled sliding doors into the front living room, was likewise divided and a bathroom stuck on from outside a window. Fortunately this renovation work was carried out with no destruction to the solid brick partitions.

In addition, she provided overnight accommodations for visitors and painted signs on the cement covered posts on either side of the front entrance soliciting patronage for her "hotel accommodations."

These moves proved at least successful enough to enable her to meet her most pressing needs. People enjoyed staying there, both because of the house itself and because they instinctively came to like Reinette and her strange bohemian ways.

One of our older lawyers of the state once told me that he would call Reinette weeks in advance to make his reservations to stay overnight when he came to Tallahassee to argue a case before the Supreme Court. "I found her absolutely delightful," he said. "No matter what time I arrived, even if late at night, she would wait up to greet me. I can see her now. She was a big woman and usually dressed in loose-fitting things that flowed and trailed behind when she moved. She would come to the door herself to receive me, always with a warm greeting. After I got settled in my room upstairs she would insist that I come back down for a 'little tea or coffee.' It often turned out to be neither, but something with much more authority. We then sat together and talked. Sometimes she smoked a cigar, of all things, lounging on an old chaise that she had made comfortable from years of individual form-fitting. I enjoyed listening to her; then she would insist that I tell her any 'spicy' news I had and, anticipating this, I was usually prepared."

Reinette launched project after project to make money, but none of these turned out as she had visualized. Once a visitor talked her into a scheme for making and bottling a homemade sauce, something like catsup but much more exciting. The visitor supplied the know-how in exchange for free room rent. Robert Aldridge pitched in and Reinette was the director of operations. They bought tomatoes in large quantities from everywhere they could find them. They were green when purchased and the timing of the ripening was one of the elements of great importance to the enterprise. They advertised that they would buy glass bottles of all sizes and shapes for a penny each delivered at The Grove. Children and older people started coming in with wheelbarrows and wagons loaded with bottles—long-neck bottles, and no-neck bottles, dirty bottles and clean bottles, fat ones and skinny ones—they all came pouring in. The cleaning and sterilizing proceeded under David's direction, while Robert and Reinette prepared the ingredients and did the cooking.

The operation went off very successfully—at first. The sauce was cooked, it tasted good, and went into hundreds of bottles.

What they had not reckoned with, however, was the matter of distribution. No one was in charge of sales. So they had bottles filled with sauce and stoppers all in place but nowhere to put them. They wound up stacking them on the back porch of the main house. With their merchandise thus warehoused, they felt they could then go forth and concentrate on a selling campaign. But before the sales campaign got into gear, there was a totally unexpected development.

Late at night, Reinette was awakened by the sound of

an explosion, followed by another, and then another. She hurried downstairs, and by this time the back porch sounded like a giant popcorn popper. The bottles of sauce were popping their stoppers and as the stoppers popped the red stuff inside popped out too and the porch floor, ceiling, and all—were streaked and splattered. Aldridge had gotten there first. Clad in pajamas, he was wading barefoot in the flowing red tide, nonchalantly surveying the scene at close range.

"Robert, what on earth is happening?" Reinette stormed.

"Why, it is simply a case of too much fermentation," he calmly replied.

"What do you mean," Reinette pursued him.

"Well, I felt that a bit of the wine I had would add to the flavor and quality, so I varied the recipe slightly. Now, it appears, our corks just do not fit tightly enough!"

With Reinette's involvement in money-making schemes, the grounds of The Grove were almost completely left to nature, and the briers and brambles out-dueled the Cherokee roses and honeysuckle. This gave the place an appearance of neglect and decadence.

Reinette continued to fall further behind in meeting her obligations, and a cousin, Mr. John W. Ford, of Youngstown, came to her rescue with advances aggregating some $17,000. She gave him a mortage on The Grove property to secure the repayment of these loans.

Once Reinette noticed that some of the copper down spouts from the roof gutters had been pulled off and were no longer to be seen. When she questioned David he told her that "Mr. Dick," Reinette's brother who was also living at The Grove, had pulled them off, taken them downtown and sold them for money "to buy a bottle of whiskey with."

Mr. and Mrs. E. N. Brown of Tallahassee had become her closest friends in Tallahassee. Mr. Brown was experienced in developing real estate, and when Reinette reached an almost unmanageable debt situation in 1939,

The Grove, circa 1939.

Courtesy of FSU Library

she solicited Mr. Brown's help in devising a last resort plan
to sell off Grove lands surrounding the big house. Together, they worked out a plotted division covering Block
"A", the main house; Block "B", which included lots num-
bered 1 through 13, inclusive; Block "C", and Block "D",
which included the three small cottages to the rear of the
main house. Reinette had agreed that Mr. Brown would
have his choice of one of the lots in exchange for his services in working out the subdivision plans. The hope was
that the lots would bring enough money to pay off the
mortage to Mr. Ford which covered all of the property.
With more irony of truth than humor she exclaimed once:
"I feel like an octopus who is sustaining himself by eating
his own tentacles one by one."

Before this subdivision plan could be consummated,

Reinette became seriously ill. The cause of her illness is unknown, but I am inclined to think that in the quiet of her big house she felt the impact of what this plan of selling lots would mean in the way of destruction to the essential character of The Grove as a home.

To have a road branching off her front driveway and encircling her house, with all sorts of new houses built facing toward her home from whose porches strangers could peer into her house, was a prospect which must have forced her into a deep sense of despair. This was the expansive front yard where, when the little city of Tallahassee had proudly celebrated its centennial in 1924, the pageant of Indian lore and the founding of the city in 1824 was performed. And this was the pageant for which she had written the script. She must have found the thought of this land now being desecrated by strange houses and yards and people unbearable.

They took her to the little Johnstons Hospital, a few blocks to the east, which was then the best hospital in the city. There she lived out the balance of her days, passing on October 30, 1940.

In her will, which was duly probated, she appointed Mr. Brown to serve as executor. The Grove was devised to her cousin, Mr. Ford, and to his sister, Miss Adler, because of their kindnesses and to satisfy her debts. Numerous items of silver, paintings, furniture, and the like were given to those to whom she felt especially close, including relatives from both her mother's and her father's families. She gave to Robert Aldridge, her Panacea cottage. To her faithful servant, David Floyd, she bequeathed some furniture and the cow he had looked after for her.

In the receipt the executor obtained from David, he certifies receipt of the "piece of furniture provided under item twenty of the will." Then there is added the poignant notation, "cow mentioned in will is dead."

Reinette was buried by the side of her grandmother in the family cemetery behind The Grove. Her grave was left unmarked when the estate was finally settled. Mr. Brown explained there was not enough money left after all claims were met with which to buy a stone.

In Reinette's pageant commemorating the founding of Tallahassee in 1824, woven into a little Indian love story, she tells of the meeting of Commissioners Williams and Simmons in search of a place to locate the Florida territorial capital and of the negotiations with the Indians that ensued. Honor is also paid to the heroic boys of West Florida Seminary for their valiant fight to save the capital from capture by the Union forces during the Civil War.

The last scene is described to be in the "Ballroom at the old Call Mansion during Administration of Governor Call." There follows a mystical dream of social life at that time and warm tributes to Indians and to the West Florida Seminary, narrated by characters portraying "Vision," "Memory," "Pioneer Spirit," "Adventure." The last lines are Reinette's poetic tribute to "Memory":

> "We are apt to forget the hardships, struggles and discouragements of those early days.
>
> "It is left to me, the Spirit of Memory, to cherish the legends of our land.
>
> "The sweet spirit of Vision will fade,
>
> "But I, Memory will come back again to recall to those who take too lightly amid the luxuries and comforts of today,
>
> "The struggle of those, who, sustained by the strength and power of Omnipotent Love and Intelligence,
>
> "Have hewn the way before us, making possible our fair city of Tallahassee
>
> "Let our Centennial be our feast day, and celebrated with song and dance, as did the brave Seminoles their Buskita."

In the House of Call, Reinette Long Hunt is indeed a legend never to be forgotten as long as "Memory" holds sway.

MARY CALL III
(Revival and Renewal)

When Reinette Hunt's pageant was being presented in the yard of The Grove in 1924, one of the observers, a seventh grader, was Mary Call Darby. This young girl with dark brown, wavy hair falling down her back to her waist, a face with large brown eyes that were direct and steady as she talked, a nose that was distinctively straight and well-proportioned, and small dimples which appeared high over her cheekbones when she smiled, would never be lost in any crowd.

Her mother, Jane Brevard Darby, also was in the group gathered around to watch the pageant, but she had eyes almost wholly for her own.

Mrs. Darby and her daughter were descendants of Mary Call, the youngest daughter of General and Mrs. Call. The control of The Grove had come down through the older daughter, Ellen, and her descendants. But Mary and her children and grandchildren had been no less interested in it, even though less closely associated.

Mary and her family were never dependent on The Grove as Ellen and her descendants were. They were more successful on their own, though they had many economic and other difficulties.

She and Theodore Washington Brevard were married in Tallahassee when both were 27 years of age. Her husband bore the same name as his father who was a descendant of the family of Brevards who were prominent in the development of North Carolina during the colonial period. The father had practiced law first in Charleston, South Carolina, then moved to Alabama in 1833 where he became a distinguished young judge. Son Theodore was born in Alabama, but the family moved to Florida in 1847 and settled in Tallahassee. The father became comptroller of Florida and made an outstanding twelve-year record in this office. Brevard County, Florida, was named in his honor.

Mary Call (Darby) Collins and her mother, Jane (Brevard) Darby.

Son Theodore, Mary's husband, went to school at Mercer College in Georgia, then was graduated in law from the University of Virginia. He began his practice in Tallahassee where he and his wife, Mary Call, raised their family. He was an exceptionally able lawyer-soldier during the Civil War, advancing to the rank of brigadier general. He was captured by Union forces three days before Lee's surrender and spent five months in prison before returning to Tallahassee to resume his life with his family and his legal career. General Brevard was elected to represent Leon County in the State Senate soon after his return, thus resuming a legislative service which had been started before the war. His brilliant career was ended with his sudden death, presumably from a heart attack in Tallahassee in 1882, at the age of forty-seven.

This was, of course, a tragic blow to his wife, Mary Call, and their children. These included a son, Richard Call who never married; a son, Ephraim Mays who became a prominent Tallahassee doctor; a daughter, Caroline Mays, who never married, but became the state's first truly competent historian. (She authored a History of Florida which was the standard textbook used in the schools covering this subject for many decades. She was recognized as a distinguished teacher of Florida State College for Women, subsequently Florida State University. A prominent elementary school of Tallahassee was named in her honor and the first local chapter of the Daughters of the American Revolution bears her name).

A daughter, Alice, was married to Dr. George H. Gwynn of Tallahassee. (They had one son, George H. Gwynn, Jr. and, tragically, Alice lost her life when he was born. The child was taken in to live with the Brevards and grew up with his grandmother, Mary Call. He was graduated from the medical school of the University of Maryland and was a prominent doctor practicing in Tallahassee until his death in 1956.)

Theodore Washington Brevard.

A daughter, Jane Kirkman met and fell in love with State Senator Thomas A. Darby, who came to Tallahassee from Putnam County, where he had substantial citrus and land investments. He had been married previously in North Carolina and his first wife had died. He was a man of unusual talents and varied interests, mostly dealing with business developments related to natural resources. He had mining interests in Alaska at the time of his marriage in Tallahassee and took his bride to Alaska for their honeymoon. He had a seat on the New York Stock Exchange

Mary (Call) Brevard.

where he was compelled to spend most of his time. He speculated in oil and was the organizer of several exploration companies.

During their later years together, Jane kept her primary base in Tallahassee with her mother, but she would visit New York often and Mr. Darby would visit Tallahassee often. They lived in New York five years after their marriage, and it was here that Mary Call III was born. Soon afterward, however, the doctor advised that a warmer climate would be better for the new baby's health and the

Thomas A. Darby.

family returned to Tallahassee and to Jane's mother's home.

Mr. Darby was a speculator and his fortune rose and fell. He would become quite rich, then lose everything in his next venture. He had the style and manners of a well-born man and a well-banked one. He had excellent tastes and the gifts he brought from New York to his wife and child were always beautiful beyond anything seen in Tallahassee. He was a visionary, ahead of his time always. He loved to argue and could well support and articulate his strong views. He developed a plan for producing and marketing the South's cotton crop which would have been eagerly accepted in the later Roosevelt era, but it was too far advanced for his time. Sadly, on the eve of what he thought would be his greatest success, he died suddenly in a New York hotel from a heart attack, leaving his widow and child no inheritance of substantial material value.

Mary Call Brevard had a strong sense of family solidarity. Her home was a large frame house on North Monroe Street, a block south of The Grove. There she raised the infant, George Gwynn, Jr., after his mother died. There, under her wing, she kept Caroline Brevard and Jane Brevard Darby with her daughter, Mary Call. Doctor Brevard had his home independently, but his association with his mother and sisters continued to be a very close one. After young George Gwynn married and was practicing medicine on his own, his grandmother also kept his family there.

Jane had only one mission in life after Senator Darby's death—to raise and care for their daughter, Mary Call. To this end, she gave total priority in her means and efforts. Mrs. Darby was not the gregarious type. Like her mother, she was serious in purpose—faithful to her beliefs in the highest standards of human conduct. She preferred the company of her family above all. To lie, cheat, or steal was grossly immoral; but no more so than more subtle forms of sin such as to deceive, to envy, or to hate. She was well-grounded in the liberal arts pattern of education. The whole family were avid readers and history was their most important subject. They read the Sunday edition of the *New York Times* every week, the *National Geographic* every month. They understood well what was going on throughout the nation and the world. Young Mary Call Darby was carefully directed in this pattern.

The family was a proud one. They emphasized quality

The Brevard home, corner of Monroe and Brevard Streets, Tallahassee.

in things they acquired, not quantity; basic values in their
beliefs, not impressions. They were greatly respected in
Tallahassee. This was because they were part of a proud
old family heritage, and their manner of life commanded
respect.

Much sorrow came to those Mary Call Brevard brought
to live in her household. Richard Call died in 1918. She,
herself, and Caroline were stricken in the influenza epi-
demic of 1920 and both died within a few days of each
other in that year. Young Dr. George Gwynn and his wife
lost three of their six children while living there. Only
Jane Darby with her daughter, Mary Call, and the Gwynns
remained at the end of 1929. Then, in 1930, Jane died and
19-year-old Mary Call, a junior at Florida State College
for Women, moved into the home of her uncle, Dr. E. M.
Brevard, about three blocks south on Monroe Street. The
Gwynns built and moved into their own home three years

later and the old "Brevard" house on Monroe Street fell strangely silent.

On June 29, 1932, Mary Call was married to LeRoy Collins, twenty-three-year-old "starting out" lawyer of Tallahassee. Dr. Brevard, as Mary Call's guardian, had given his consent to the marriage after exacting the agreement from both principals that Mary Call would remain in college until graduation, a bargain that was faithfully kept.

Shortly after the Gwynns moved to their own new house, Mary Call III, and I moved into the old Brevard house, thus saving rent which was of great importance in those depression years. By 1940, we had two children, LeRoy, Jr. and Jane Brevard. The lands on Lake Jackson which had descended from General Call to Mary Call, her uncle (Dr. Brevard), and her first cousin (Dr. Gwynn) were sold to John H. Phipps and the proceeds invested. We lived frugally and my law business was slowly but gradually growing downtown. I also served in the House of Representatives of the State Legislature for the sessions of 1935, 1937, and 1939.

Over all her growing years, Mary Call had been nurtured on the stories and history surrounding The Grove. Whether by any specific design of her mother or not, there was created in Mary Call a longing that someday she could live and raise her family there. It hurt her to see the physical deterioration that was taking place. From time to time we strolled up to the Grove and talked of the future. "Roy, someday we ought to get this house. We could do so much with it," Mary Call often confided, though we did not dream then that it could happen.

After Reinette died and it was learned that the property had been devised to Mr. Ford, we made an effort to buy it from him. Mr. Ford was a sensitive, kind person, and said that he realized that the "property should stay in the family." We had made him aware of our financial limitations and after considerable thought he told us one day that he and his sister would make a sale to us if we could

LeRoy and Mary Call (Darby) Collins, circa 1934.

pay him enough to permit him to recover his loans to Reinette and interest and also what he had to advance to pay off other debts of the estate. We thought we could arrange this and the prospect was most exciting.

Then it was learned that other Tallahasseeans were interested.

Among these were Payne H. Midyette and Jack W. Simmons, both close friends, and Justice Alto Adams, who had recently come to Tallahassee for service on the State Supreme Court. All were wealthy, and this was chilling and depressing news. There would be no chance for us to match what any one of them could offer. But then, as if fate was taking a hand in the matter, when they learned of Mary Call's interest, each, in a most generous and understanding way, took the firm position that he would not offer her any competition. What a wonderful spirit!

A trade was made with Mr. Ford. With the use of funds belonging to Mary Call from the Phipps sale, and some of mine, and a loan for which both of us became indebted, The Grove ownership changed and as proud new owners we moved in early in 1941.

Mary Call had established certain priorities as owner. Number one was to paint over the sign "Hotel Accommodations" on the concrete entrance posts. This was done, with all the family and some friends participating, within thirty minutes. Other things took longer: the bathrooms had to come off the living and dining rooms and the beaver board partitions had to come out; furniture had to be moved from the Brevard house; bad roof leaks had to be repaired; everything had to be washed and cleaned; and these were just the beginning.

Money was not available to pay for help and much of the work was done by the owners themselves. The grounds had gotten almost beyond the hope of reclaiming, but we dug, and hacked, and raked, and sprigged, as best we could.

It was at this stage one day when Mary Call came into the reception room of my law office. I was busy with a client and she sat to wait. Later, Charles Ausley, a partner, came into the reception room just as I joined Mary Call there, and exclaimed exuberantly to both of us: "Well, how are the Master and Mistress of The Grove today?" To which modest Mary Call replied, "Master and Mistress nothing, you mean the grubber and the hoer." All those in the office who heard this discreetly managed not to laugh, but after I had quickly pulled Mary Call into my private office, we could hear the bursts of laughter from the reception office.

Mary Call got something with The Grove she did not bargain for—Robert Aldridge. He had the most unbelievable conflicts in his traits of personality and character. He was a gentleman, yet a rascal. He was highly literate, yet most of the work he did could be done by an illiterate. He was effusive in his commitments to do specific things, yet undependable in doing anything as planned. On occasions that suited him, his dress and manners were impeccable, yet he was completely comfortable with the talk and boorishness of the most disadvantaged common laborer.

When we moved into The Grove, he was occupying the front end of the basement hall behind a boarded-up wall, and we had no idea what he had with him in the space he had separated off for his own. But Mary Call became suspicious when her keen nose detected a musty alcoholic odor coming out. While he was away one day she peeped in and discovered that his cot, wash basin, and other essentials, were sandwiched in between kegs and barrels, most of which were clearly involved in the process of wine and home brew production.

He was very friendly and courtly when Mary Call suggested that he move to one of the old cottages in the rear of the big house. (Since he knew where everything was at The Grove, how to change the fuses, where all the leaks were, and the vintage and faults of every appliance in the house we actually considered him indispensable.) He came to me soon after this and with a formal manner said: "Sir, if I take the cottage, I think I should pay you a reasonable rent for its use."

"No," I said, "You are going to help us and we will be glad for you to use the cottage rent free."

"I would not consider such a thing. This should be on a business basis," he countered.

"What then do you think it will be worth to you," I asked. "I should say $30 per month would be fair," he replied.

"I think this is too much," I said. Then I said, "Why don't we settle for half that, $15 per month."

Aldridge smiled and nodding said, "If you will be sat-isfied with that, it will be fine with me, I just believe we should keep our relations on a sound business basis."

"Agreed," I said. And he went on his way.

He stayed there for several years after that—and never paid the first cent under this rental agreement so carefully arrived at. The subject of rent was never brought up by either of us again.

In the dining room we kept a cabinet with doors opening down to the floor in which wine was stored. Mary Call had suspected that Mr. Aldridge had discovered this and had secretly made some raids, using water to replace what he took from the bottles. She wrote him a polite note placing it in a prominent place atop one of the bottles in the cabi-net asking him kindly to discontinue this practice. She thought if he was not guilty he would never see the note; if guilty, he would see it and, she hoped, would discon-tinue his raiding without an embarrassing confrontation.

He saw it all right. We knew this because suddenly he became very wounded and offended in his nature in our presence. He sulked and did not want to talk to us. We checked and found the note was gone.

When this episode had time to be forgotten, one day Mary Call had come back earlier than she told Aldridge to expect her from a trip downtown. She opened the door from the hall into the dining room to get the vacuum cleaner, and was shocked to see there on his knees in front of the cabinet Robert, holding one of the bottles of wine in his hand and just before taking a swig.

"Oh, excuse me, I'm sorry," Mary Call said before she realized it, "I just wanted to get the vacuum cleaner."

"That's quite all right, let me get it for you," Aldridge said, as he gallantly rose, returned the bottle, closed the cabinet and picked up the vacuum cleaner. The incident was never mentioned again.

Other experiences crowd in when Aldridge comes to mind. Out in his separate cottage he had quite a happy life. It was a very old and run down shack. At one place a brick pillar underneath had given way and that whole end of the house was badly sagging. I asked him why he didn't repair it and expressed the feeling that it might be dangerous. With a straight face he proceeded to tell me that he had a cup of water on his stove inside and that when the house gave way to the extent that the water would spill out of the cup, he would then know a point of danger had been reached and that he must do something about it.

He had a favorite cat and once I saw two dead squirrels on his door step. When I asked him how they got there he explained that his cat cared so much for him that she would kill the squirrels and bring them in for him to clean and cook and for both of them to eat. Once Mary Call and I made a call on him to see just what things were like inside his house. The house was full of boxes, cans, crates, and all sorts of objects, with cleared paths one had to use in getting from place to place. There was a paper sack hanging from the ceiling on a string and when I asked him about it he explained that he kept his bread in the sack to protect it from the rats! Evidently, the rats couldn't come down that string. Also, Mary Call noticed a pair of elegant shoe trees on which he had carefully placed his old tennis shoes that he used in his roofing work.

It was not long after this visit when the local paper carried the story that several cases of typhus fever had been found in the city and that this contagious disease was carried by rats. This set Mary Call off on a determined effort to eradicate Mr. Aldridge's rats. Whatever she asked him to do about cleaning his place up he agreed to do, but never did.

Finally she came up with a very clever plan. He was almost always home on Saturday afternoons, so she called the city sanitary inspector up to The Grove early one Saturday afternoon and explained that she wanted him to go down and inspect Mr. Aldridge's cottage without Aldridge knowing he had been requested to do so by her.

"Now, I know it is a dirty, filthy place and I want you

to tell him so and give him a specific time in which he must clean it up."

The inspector agreed to cooperate fully and we watched him march manfully down to the house and enter. Then we waited, and waited, and waited, not understanding why it should take the inspector so long to complete his mission. Finally, after about an hour he came out. He was reeling and rocking in high, good humor with Robert right behind him slapping his back insisting that he come back again soon. Mary Call took a few steps toward them aghast.

Then the inspector said gaily, "Don't you worry Mrs. Collins, everything is fine down here, just fine."

Without a word Mary Call turned abruptly and went back into her own house. Evidently, Aldridge had made a new friend with the discreet use of some of the products of his extraordinary kitchen supplementing his other personal charms.

Robert Aldridge, with all his eccentricities and the frustrations that followed in his wake, was a good man, and a good friend. We could have no doubt of that when we learned first hand of his devotion to The Grove. That something about the house that affected most people whose lives it touched, got to him and held him tightly. The Grove gave something to him and he returned the affection generously and faithfully.

Beyond cleaning, painting, and clearing out obstructions there were many other needs for work on the house. The back porch was falling off from age and poor maintenance. Mary Call wanted to make this area more functional and with the help of David Biers of Atlanta, a glassed-in porch, with a new kitchen for the main floor and two bathrooms above for the bedrooms, were planned. It was an expensive job but necessary to give a growing family a space for normal "Florida" room use. The prior makeshift kitchen on the basement floor was almost impossible to use for serving the main floor dining room. We kept the original plan of the back porch ceiling, and the same dimensions as the old porch, but put in a suspended brick floor, and glass windows reaching from floor to ceiling. Since then this area has borne a large share of day-in, day-out family use, sparing the central, main floor hallway and adjoining rooms much wear and tear. It has made the back door the main entrance so far as traffic is concerned.

The furnishings Mary Call had in her part of the family possessions were, of course, inadequate for such a large house, and we were determined to acquire more pieces as we were able to do so. By good fortune, we came to know Mr. James Cogar, a teacher of eighteenth century furnishings at William and Mary College in Virginia, and former curator of the Williamsburg Restoration. Mr. Cogar took a deep interest in The Grove when he came and saw it. He agreed to buy in England and Scotland some old pieces which would be beautiful and authentic. This was the beginning of a long, personal relationship which has resulted in an appropriate furnishing of most of the house with original pieces. The furniture, though costly, was acquired at a cost of only a small fraction of its value today.

As a part of the restoration of The Grove we were extremely anxious to have returned, if possible, the three items which Ellen Call is known to have sold to Mr. Flagler—the stones from Fort San Marcos (St. Marks), the portrait of Jackson, and the field desk of Jackson. We first sought the cooperation of the Flagler heirs through Judge James R. Knott, circuit judge of West Palm Beach, a close friend with whom we grew up as youngsters in Tallahassee. Judge Knott knew well Mrs. Jean Flagler Matthews, granddaughter of Mr. Flagler, who lives in Palm Beach and who was then developing Whitehall, Flagler's magnificent home in Palm Beach, into a public museum.

Arrangements were made by the Judge for negotiations in Palm Beach between Mrs. Matthews and me. As it turned out, however, there was no report of this purchase in Mr. Flagler's records and after a diligent search we were advised that no trace could be found of any of the three items.

However, later I found the stones imbedded in the wall of the beautiful large patio of Whitehall. They were almost completely covered with vines and evidently their presence had long been forgotten.

They remain there to this day. While over the years a friendly relationship has continued to exist between Mrs. Matthews and us, she has not yet agreed to the removal and return of the stones. We haven't lost hope that she will some day.

Frankly, we have not expected to keep the stones at The Grove where they stayed for so long. It has been our desire that some day the old fort at St. Marks could be rebuilt as nearly possible as it was in 1753, and the ancient corner stones with their still legible carvings put into their original places again. The plans from which the fort was built are available for such a reconstruction and the ruins with the original foundations can still be easily observed. We believe it would take only a good effort to raise privately the needed funds for such a project, and that having the original stones to use would be a helpful rallying influence.

When I was elected governor of Florida in 1954, our family moved into the Governor's Mansion located immediately south of The Grove property between First Avenue and Brevard Street. (It was a part of The Grove property before it was sold off by Ellen Call Long and later conveyed to the state.) The house there was badly deteriorated and engineers soon advised that it was dangerous for occupancy. So we moved back across the street and for two years The Grove served again as a governor's family and official home. Offices were prepared in the basement for home work, and The Grove took on a full normal load of social, political, and family use.

During this two year absence the state built a new governor's residence on the spot the old one had occupied

Entrance hall, The Grove, 1971.

across the street. It was very similar in exterior design to the Hermitage of Jackson in Tennessee. Mary Call spent much of her time in selecting the furnishings, working directly with the State Commission given this responsibility. When the construction work and furnishing were completed we moved from The Grove to the beautiful new mansion.

After the family returned, the State Cabinet called on the Commission, which had been set up by law to supervise the furnishing of the new mansion,* to ascertain and recommend a fair amount which the state should pay us for the use of The Grove during the two years in which it was used. As I recall the amount of $9,000 was recommended, and I anticipated applying this sum to the mort-

*Members of this Commission were: Mr. Frank D. Moor, Mrs. John H. Phipps, Mr. William Watson, Mrs. Rod Shaw Sr., Mrs. J. Edwin White, Mrs. Tom Bailey and Mrs. LeRoy Collins.

Living room, The Grove, 1971.

gage indebtedness The Grove was carrying, but Mary Call would not consider accepting the tender.

"We just wouldn't feel right about accepting rent for living in our own house," she said. "Besides, we and the place itself, were happy to be able to meet this state need." And that was that. She won the argument hands down.

As The Grove had changed, so had the family of its owners. LeRoy, Jr. was seven when the Collinses moved in. A daughter, Jane Brevard, was five. The fourth Mary Call was six months. Our fourth child, Darby, a daughter, was born in 1950.

My work since has involved travel in various pursuits including service in the Navy in World War II, and in Washington following our second term as governor. This has meant that our family has been away from The Grove from time to time for some protracted absences. But it has been home for all of us since Mr. Ford said "yes." We have owned it and it has owned us, as General Call predicted it would.

While we were in Washington, we once tried to open the main floor to the public for regularly scheduled tours. In this we had the special help of Mr. Cogar, Rev. William Harris, then a practicing lawyer, and Mrs. DeVere Burr, a friend whose place adjoins The Grove. But the venture did not prove profitable and when the Internal Revenue Service questioned our right for loss deductions, this was abandoned. The little ticket house is still in place as a sort of memorial to a good motive but poor business judgment.

We have purchased two pieces of land on the strip between The Grove property, as originally acquired and Monroe Street on the east. One of the parcels is 100 feet in width, the other 66 feet. The 66 foot unimproved parcel was purchased in 1967 and cost more than the entire property (ten acres and the big house) cost in 1941.

In *Florida Breezes,* Mrs. Long not only describes social life in the town of Tallahassee, but she places just as much emphasis on life on the great plantations to the north and east. Understandably, she speaks in warm and glowing terms of her father's plantation at Lake Jackson. She quotes Governor Call as saying of his farm lands:

> "It is the prettiest place in all Florida, and I feel it is a day lost, when compelled to leave it. This and the surrounding country, were favorite lands of the Spaniards and English. The Chiefs, 'Wild Cat,' and Econchatinico, have told me how older Indians told them of many settlements on these high lands, sloping to the lake, and so near that you could hear the cocks crow from one to the other. On the Ochilochee, or Orchard Pond plantation, there are still the remains of a Spanish town, or rather, the debris, to show where it stood."

A source of enormous benefit and pleasure for Mary Call and for me over the years has been our association with the "plantation people" who have developed large hunting and nature preserves with beautiful homes, north and east of Tallahassee. These primarily seasonal settlers from "up North", for generations have appreciated the natural beauty of our region and because of their love for the land have applied their enthusiasm and means to protect and enhance it. They have long been a vanguard for the more recent surge of broad public interest in ecological values. They have developed extensive programs of soil care and for the propagation of wild life (quail, turkey, dove and fresh water fish, in the main) thus providing for themselves and their guests some of the finest hunting in the world.

It is remarkable how they have made it possible for large areas of these lands to continue almost in the same condition they were when the Indians roamed and hunted over them. It is appropriate too that they have revived and continued many of the Indian names like Welaunee and Ayavalla. Other names from the early Spanish settlement of the territory have been preserved also, like El Destino.

As by-products of the plantation owners' interest and investments, they and their guests have helped to broaden the horizons of many local people. Certainly this has been true for Mary Call and for me. We number many of them among our close friends. And among our fondest memories are stimulating, joyous occasions we have been privileged to share with them.*

In the later part of 1961, while living in Washington, when I was serving as president of the National Association of Broadcasters, Mary Call was asked to become a vice regent of The Mount Vernon Ladies Association and

---

* Among those we have seen most often have been Mrs. George F. Baker, Sr., Mr. and Mrs. John H. Phipps, Mr. and Mrs. Sheldon Whitehouse, Mrs. Alexandria McKay, Mrs. Alfred B. Maclay; Senator and Mrs. Walter E. Edge; and Colonel and Mrs. Lloyd C. Griscom. These have taken a very special interest in The Grove, visiting often, bringing their visitors, and helping us in countless ways to preserve as well as enjoy it. Years ago Mrs. Baker realized that our oil portrait of Mary Call Brevard which hangs over the dining room mantle, had become dark and torn. She generously offered to have this repaired for us and took it personally to a friend of hers at the Metropolitan Museum in New York who did a beautiful job of restoration.

accepted the appointment. This organization was formed back in 1853. It owns, maintains, and supervises Mount Vernon, George Washington's beautiful homeplace, overlooking the Potomac. Only one vice regent can come from any one state and each serves for life. Mary Call loves this work. Each year in the fall the vice regents assemble at Mount Vernon where they are housed for a week, and re-experience some of the charm and grace of life that Washington maintained there. There is work to do, reports on the year's experiences both in providing the opportunity for the public to visit there, and in the always continuing search to find, acquire, and bring back to Mount Vernon the original items of furniture and furnishings that General and Mrs. Washington placed there. Nothing else is purchased. Regardless of how beautiful or appropriate in style and period, it cannot be at Mount Vernon unless it was actually there when the house was lived in by the Washingtons.

These fall meetings are strictly for the ladies. This is the same organization in which it was suggested that Mrs. Ellen Call Long accept membership in the late 1860s. Mrs. Long had declined with the suggestion that Madam Murat be elected instead, and this suggestion was followed later.

The little cemetery behind the grove was always high on Mary Call's priorities and within a few months after we came to The Grove we erected a stone marking the grave of Reinette Long Hunt. When Robert Aldridge died in 1951 we wanted him to be buried there too. He had lived there and been such a part of the struggle to maintain the house and such a friend of the owners, over a span of thirty years, that we felt strongly that it would be the right and proper thing to do. But the city would not allow this. It was ruled that only members of the family could ever be buried in the plot—no exceptions.

Back in the early 1930s Reinette Hunt and the other members of the Call family became alarmed about a rumor which came to her that the City of Tallahassee planned to extend North Adams Street (which dead-ended at The Grove entrance,) around the main house then over the cemetery, to connect with the extension of Adams Street north from Third Avenue. They were advised that this could be blocked if Mrs. Hunt would deed the cemetery to Jackson Lodge No. 1 of the Free and Accepted Masons (Tallahassee). The Masons were deeply interested because Governor Call had not only been an ardent member but had served as grand master of the Grand Lodge of Florida in 1850.

A deed to the plot was executed by Mrs. Hunt in 1934, and thus, technical control of the plot passed out of the family.

In 1959, with the sympathetic and friendly cooperation of Mr. J. Lewis Hall of Tallahassee, former Grand Master of the Grand Lodge of Florida, this title was returned. A plaque was placed on the edge of the cemetery which reads:

> "This cemetery was deeded by the Call family to Jackson Lodge No. 1 F & A M of Florida, May 11, 1934, and cared for and protected for 25 years, and then was conveyed to Mrs. Mary Call Darby Collins, great-granddaughter of Richard K. Call, in recognition of her deep interest in this hallowed spot and with full assurance of its permanent protection by the Call family."

Florida's long time outstanding Justice and Chief Justice of the State Supreme Court, Glenn Terrell, who had been a close friend of my family since my childhood, asked me once if I was aware of Mary Call's Florida political background. I replied that I thought so but was anxious to learn more. Then the Justice said "Did you realize that one of her great-grandfathers [R. K. Call] was twice a governor; that another was a state comptroller [Theodore Washington Brevard]; that her grandfather was a state senator [T. W. Brevard]; that her cousin was a U.S. senator and judge [Wilkinson Call]; that her father was a state senator [T. A. Darby]; and that her husband was a state legislator and governor [L. Collins]." Justice Terrell, who gave me the oath of office at my first inauguration as governor, then said: "I don't know of anyone in Florida who has a heritage of public service like that!"

About a year prior to the ending of my last term as governor, one evening a group of close friends, mostly officials I had depended upon heavily in our administration, were with me in a very informal work session at the executive offices at the mansion. After all the business discussions were over a friendly man-to-man talk session developed. One of those present suggested that since under the constitution I could not seek another term it would be fine if the state could have a continuity of programs and administration by another plan. "What you should do, Governor, is get Mary Call to run! She could get elected then you could carry on, stamping her name on the orders instead of your own."

Everyone present laughed, then I said with mock seriousness: "You know, that might be possible but I don't think it would work for three reasons: (1) it is time for the people to elect a new Governor, (2) six years is long enough for one man to serve in this job consecutively, and (3) if Mary Call got elected *she would be the Governor* regardless of what anybody else might plan. These are my reasons for saying 'No' gentlemen but not necessarily in that order!"

The Grove, 1971.

Bibliography

Beater, Jack. *Tales of South Florida and the Thousand Islands.* Fort Myers, Fla., The Author, 1964.

Boyd, Mark F. "The Joint Operations of the Federal Army and Navy Near St. Marks, Florida, March 1865," *Florida Historical Quarterly,* XXIX (Oct. 1950), 96–124.

Butler, Pierce. *Judah P. Benjamin.* Philadelphia. G. W. Jacobs & Co., 1907.

Dodd, Dorothy. "The Wrecking Business on the Florida Reef, 1822–1860," *Florida Historical Quarterly,* XXII (Apr. 1944), 171–199.

Doherty, Herbert J., Jr. *Richard Keith Call, Southern Unionist.* Gainesville, University of Florida Press, 1961.

Grady, Henry W. "Colonel R. A. Alston," *The Florida Mirror* (Fernandina), Mar. 29, 1879.

Hanna, Alfred J. *Flight into Oblivion.* Richmond, Va., Johnson Publishing Co., 1938.

Laumer, Frank. *Massacre!* Gainesville, University of Florida Press, 1968.

Long, Ellen Call. *Florida Breezes, or Florida New and Old.* 1883. Margaret L. Chapman, ed. Gainesville, University of Florida Press, facsimile reprint, 1962.

Meade, Robert D. *Judah P. Benjamin, Confederate Statesman.* New York, Oxford University Press, 1943.

Osceola Double Number, *Florida Historical Quarterly,* XXXIII (Jan.-Apr. 1955), 161–305.

Proctor, Samuel. *Napoleon Bonaparte Broward, Florida's Fighting Democrat.* Gainesville, University of Florida Press, 1950.

Redfearn, Daniel H. "The Croom Case, 7 *Fla.* 81–205," *Florida Law Journal,* XXIII (Nov. 1949), 298–301.

———. "Presumption as to Order of Death in a Common Disaster: The Steamboat *Home,*" *Florida Bar Journal,* XXXVII (Feb. 1963), 78–99.

———. " 'The Steamboat Home'—Presumption as to Order of Death in a Common Calamity," *Florida Law Journal,* IX (May, 1935), 405–424.

Swanberg, W. A. *Citizen Hearst.* New York, Charles Scribner's Sons, 1961.

Tebeau, Charlton W. *A History of Florida.* Coral Gables, University of Miami Press, 1971.

———. *Man in the Everglades; 2,000 Years of Human History in the Everglades National Park.* Coral Gables, University of Miami Press, 1964.

Willson, Minnie Moore. *Osceola, Florida's Seminole War Chieftain.* Palm Beach, Fla., Davies Pub. Co., 1931.

———. *The Seminoles of Florida.* New York, Moffat, Yard and Co., 1920.

Young, Stanley P. and Goldman, Edward A. *The Puma, Mysterious American Cat.* Washington, D.C., American Wildlife Institute, 1946.

HOUSE OF CALL

Prince Georges County, Virginia

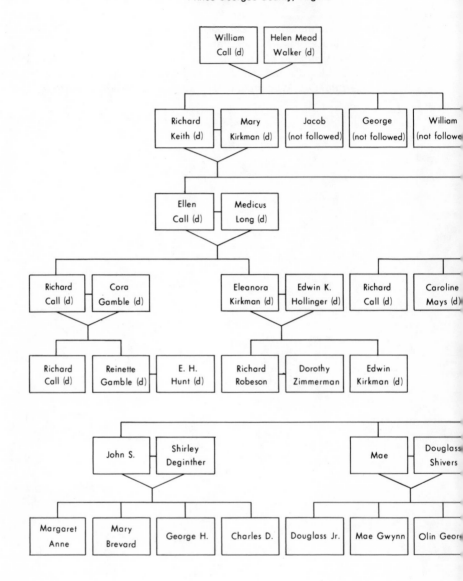

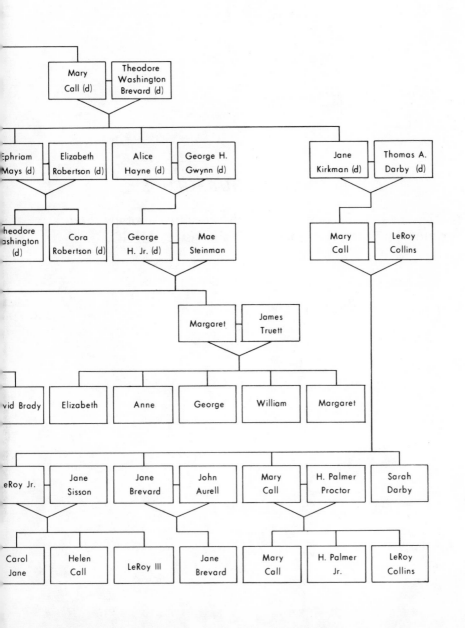

FORERUNNERS COURAGEOUS

Designed and composed in Baskerville linotype and printed by Rose Printing Co., Tallahassee, Florida

Index